LOVING
IN THE
WAR YEARS

LOVING
IN THE
WAR YEARS

CHERRÍE MORAGA

lo que nunca pasó por sus labios

south end press

The author is grateful to the New York State CAPS grant and the Mac Dowell Colony for the Arts fellowship which assisted in the completion of this work.

Some of this work previously appeared in: *IKON, Azalea, Third Woman, Lesbian Poetry: An Anthology* (Persephone Press, 1981), *Cuentos: Stories by Latinas* (Kitchen Table Press, 1983), *Conditions, Thirteenth Moon, Sinister Wisdom,* and *This Bridge Called My Back: Writings by Radical Women of Color* (Persephone Press, 1981).

other books by Cherríe Moraga:
This Bridge Called My Back: Writings by Radical Women of Color (co-editor and contributor, Persephone Press, 1981).

Cuentos: Stories by Latinas (co-editor and contributor, Kitchen Table Press, 1983).

Both books are available from Kitchen Table: Women of Color Press, Box 2753 Rockefeller Center Station, New York, New York, 10185.

Typesetting, design, and production by the South End Press Collective.
Cover design by Ellen Herman.
Library of Congress Number: 83-061474
ISBN 0-89608-195-8 (paper)
ISBN 0-89608-196-6 (cloth)

South End Press/116 Saint Botolph St./Boston, MA 02115

Para mis compañeras
especially for Barbara

for the duration.

AGRADECIMIENTOS

Gracias to all the women who helped me in the writing of this book throughout its many incarnations, most especially: Gloria Anzaldúa, Elly Bulkin, Jan Clausen, Myrtha Chabrán, Amber Hollibaugh, Deborah Geneva Leoni, Minnie Bruce Pratt, Mirtha Quintanales, and Barbara Smith.

CONTENTS

Introducción   i
The Voices of the Fallers   1

WHAT KIND OF LOVER HAVE YOU
MADE ME MOTHER?

It is You, My Sister, Who Must Be Protected   8
La Dulce Culpa   14
what is left   16

LIKE FAMILY
LOVING ON THE RUN

Pilgrimage   18
Later, She Met Joyce   19
An Open Invitation to a Meal   22
You Upset the Whole System of This Place   23
Loving on the Run   25
Loving in the War Years   29
The Slow Dance   31
Fear, A Love Poem   33
Pesadilla   36
Passage   44

VIEW OF THREE BRIDGES

Raw Experience   48
La Güera   50
For the Color of My Mother   60
It's the Poverty   62
What Does It Take?   65
Salvation, Jesus, and Suffer   67
Anatomy Lesson   68
It Got Her Over   69
Winter of Oppression, 1982   73

THE ROAD TO RECOVERY

Minds & Hearts   78
No Born-Again Children   79
November Again   81
You Call It, *Amputation*   82
For Amber   83
Heading East   85
Modern Day Hero   86
The Warbride   87

LO QUE NUNCA PASÓ POR SUS LABIOS

A Long Line of Vendidas   90
¿Donde Está Tu Rio?   145
Feed the Mexican Back Into Her   146
And Then There's Us   148
Querida Compañera   149

Glossary   150

AMAR EN LOS AÑOS DE GUERRA

Introducción

Sueño

*My lover and I are in a prison camp together.
We are in love in wartime.*

*A young soldier working as a guard has befriended us.
We ask him honestly—the truth—*are we going to die?

He answers, yes, it's almost certain. *I contemplate escaping. Ask him to help us. He blanches.* That is impossible, *he says. I regret asking him, fearing recriminations.*

I see the forest through the fence on my right. I think, the place between the trees—I could burrow through there—toward freedom? Two of us would surely be spotted. One of us has a slim chance. I think of leaving my lover, imprisoned. But immediately I understand that we must, at all costs, remain with each other. Even unto death. That it is our being together that makes the pain, even our dying, human.

Loving in the war years.

1.

Esto libro covers a span of seven years of writing. The first poems were written in 1976 when I was still in Los Angeles, living out my lesbianism as a lie on my job and a secret to my family. The two main essays of the book, "La Güera" and "A Long Line of Vendidas" were completed in 1979 and 1983, respectively.* Now I write the final introduction here in Brooklyn, New

---

* The selections are not arranged chronologically in terms of when each piece was written. Rather I have tried to create a kind of emotional/ political chronology.

York—"out-to-the-world" it feels to me to be in print.

Tonight the summer heat takes on the flavor it had when I first moved into this room—makes me tired by the thought of all this moving and working. How slow and hard change is to come. How although this book has taken me from Berkeley to San Francisco to Boston, Brooklyn, México, and back again, sigo siendo la hija de mi mamá. My mother's daughter.

My mother's daughter who at ten years old knew she was queer. Queer to believe that God cared so much about me, he intended to see me burn in hell; that unlike the other children, I was not to get by with a clean slate. I was born into this world with complications. I had been chosen, marked to *prove* my salvation. Todavía soy bien catolica—filled with guilt, passion, and incense, and the inherent Mexican faith that there is meaning to nuestro sufrimiento en el mundo.

The first time I went to the Mexican basilica where el retrato de La Virgen de Guadalupe hovers over a gilded altar, I was shocked to see that below it ran a moving escalator. It was not one that brought people up to the image that we might kiss her feet; but rather it moved people along from side to side and through as quickly as possible. A moving sidewalk built to keep the traffic going.

What struck me the most, however, was that in spite of the irreverence imposed by such technology, the most devout of the Mexican women—las pobres, few much older than me—clung to the ends of the handrailing of the moving floor, crossing themselves, gesturing besos al retrato, their hips banging up against the railing over and over again as it tried to force them off and away. They stayed. In spite of the machine. They had come to spend their time with La Virgen.

I left the church in tears, knowing how for so many years I had closed my heart to the passionate pull of such faith that promised no end to the pain. I grew white. Fought to free myself from my culture's claim on me. It seemed I had to step outside my familia to see what we as a people were doing suffering. This is my politics. This is my writing. For as much as the two have eventually brought me back to my familia, there is no fooling myself that it is my education, my "consciousness" that separated me from them. That forced me to leave home. This is what has made me the outsider so many Chicanos—very near to me in circumstance—fear.

I am a child. I watch my mamá, mis tías en una procesion cada día llegando a la puerta de mi abuela. Needing her, never doing enough for her. I remember lying on my bed midday. The sun streaming through the long window, thin sheer curtains. Next door I can hear them all. Están peleando. Mi abuela giving the cold shoulder, not giving in. Each daughter vying for a place with her. The cruel gossip. Las mentiras. My mother trying to hold onto the truth, her version of the story, su integridad.

I put my head back on the pillow and count the years this has been going on. The competition for her favor. My grandmother's control of them. I count my mother's steps as I hear her click high-heeled angry down the gravel driveway, through the fence, up the back steps. She's coming in. Estará llorando. Otra vez. I tell my sister reading a book next to me, "How many years, Jo Ann? It can't be this way for us too when we grow up."

Mi abuelita ya está muriendo muy lentamente. Cierra los ojos. Cierra la boca. El hospital le da comida por las venas. Ella no habla. No canta como cantaba. She does not squeeze my mother's hand tight in her fight against la sombra de su muerte propia. She does not squeeze the life out of her. Está durmiendo, esperando a la muerte.

And what goes with her? My claim to an internal dialogue where el gringo does not penetrate? Su memoria a de noventa y seis años going back to a time where "nuestra cultura" was not the subject of debate. *I write this book because we are losing ourselves to the gavacho. I mourn my brother in this.*

Sueño: 5 de enero 1983

My grandmother appears outside la iglesia. Standing in front as she used to do after la misa. I am so surprised that she is well enough to go out again, be dressed, be in the world. I am elated to see her—to know I get to have the feel of her again in my life.

She is, however, in great pain. She shows me her leg which has been

iii

operated on. The wound is like a huge crater in her calf—crusted, open, a gaping wound. I feel her pain so critically.

Sueño: 7 de enero 1983

En el sueño trataba de tomar yo una foto de mi abuela y de mi mamá. Mientras una mujer me esperaba en la cama. The pull and tug present themselves en mis sueños. Deseo para las mujeres/la familia. I want to take the photo of my grandmother because I know she is dying. I want one last picture. The woman keeps calling me to her bed. She wants me. I keep postponing her.

Después soñe con mi hermano. El ha regresado a la familia, not begging forgiveness, but acknowledging grievances done by him. Somos unidos.

2.

Can you go home? Do your parents know? Have they read your work? These are the questions I am most often asked by Chicanos, especially students. It's as if they are hungry to know if it's possible to have both—your own life and the life of the familia. I explain to them that sadly, this is a book my family will never see. And yet, how I wish I could share this book with them. How I wish I could show them how much I have taken them to heart—even my father's silence. What he didn't say working inside me as passionately as my mother wept it.

It is difficult for me to separate in my mind whether it is my writing or my lesbianism which has made me an outsider to my family. The obvious answer is both. For my lesbianism first brought me into writing. My first poems were love poems. That's the source—el amor, el deseo—that brought me into politics. That was when I learned my first major lesson about writing: it is the measure of my life. I cannot write what I am not willing to live up to. Is it for this reason I so often fear my own writing—fear it will jump up and push me off some precipice?

Women daily change my work. How can it be that I have always hungered for and feared falling in love as much as I do writing from my heart. Each changes you forever. Sex has

iv

always been part of the question of freedom. The freedom to want passionately. To live it out in the body of the poem, in the body of the woman. So when I feel a movement inside of me and it is a fresh drawing in of new life that I want to breathe into my work, I also feel empowered and long to be a lover like youth.

I watch my changes in the women I love.

3.

Journal Entry: 2 de julio 1982

It takes the greatest of effort to even put pen to paper—so much weighing on me. It's as if I am bankrupt of feeling, but that's not really so. My lover comes into my room, sees me face flat on the bed, gathers me into her arms. I say I am depressed and she reminds me of how I tell her so often how depression is not a feeling. Depression covers a feeling that doesn't have a chance to come out. Keeping it down. Keeping the writing back.

So often in the work on this book I felt I could not write because I have a movement on my shoulder, a lover on my shoulder, a family over my shoulder. On some level you have to be willing to lose it all to write—to risk telling the truth that no one may want to hear, even you. Not that, in fact, you *have* to lose, only that el riesgo siempre vive, threatening you.

I know with my family that even as my writing functioned to separate me from them (I cannot share my work with them), it has freed me to love them from places in myself that had before been mired in unexpressed pain. Writing has ultimately brought me back to them. They don't need this book. They have me.

The issue of being a "movement writer" is altogether different. Sometimes I feel my back will break from the pressure I feel to speak for others. A friend told me once how no wonder I had called the first book I co-edited (with Gloria Anzaldúa), "This Bridge Called My Back." *You have chronic back trouble,* she says. Funny, I had never considered this most obvious connection, all along my back giving me constant pain. And the spot that hurts the most is the muscle that controls the movement of my fingers and hands while typing. I feel it now straining at my desk.

v

Riding on the train with another friend, I ramble on about the difficulty of finishing this book, feeling like I am being asked by all sides to be a "representative" of the race, the sex, the sexuality—or at all costs to avoid that. "You don't speak for me! For the community!" My friend smiles kindly, almost amused, at me across the aisle among the sea of grey suits and businessmen. We are on the commuter train and no one would give up their single seat for us to sit together. We speak in secret code. Hablamos español.

"Ah, Chavalita," she says to me. "Tú necesitas viajar para que veas lo que en verdad es la comunidad. There's really no such thing as community among politicos. Community is simply the way people live a life together. And they're doing it all over the world. The only way to write for la comunidad is to write so completely from your heart what is your own personal truth. This is what touches people."

Some days I feel my writing wants to break itself open. Speak in a language that maybe no "readership" can follow. What does it mean that the Chicana writer if she truly follows her own voice, she may depict a world so specific, so privately ours, so full of "foreign" language to the anglo reader, there will be no publisher. The people who can understand it, don't/won't/can't read it. How can I be a writer in this? I have been translating my experience out of fear of an aloneness too great to bear. I have learned analysis as a mode to communicate what I feel the experience itself already speaks for. The combining of poetry and essays in this book is the compromise I make in the effort to be understood. In Spanish, "compromiso" is also used to mean obligation or commitment. And I guess, in fact, I write as I do because I *am committed* to communicating with both sides of myself.

I am the daughter of a Chicana and anglo. I think most days I am an embarassment to both groups. I sometimes hate the white in me so viciously that I long to forget the commitment my skin has imposed upon my life. To speak two tongues. I must. But I will not double-talk and I refuse to let *anybody's* movement determine for me what is safe and fair to say.

vi

4.

The completion of this book finds me in the heart of change. So there is no definitive statement to make here in this last piece that is to prepare you for the story of my life. For that is all this really is/can be—my story. But for whom have I tried so steadfastly to communicate? Who have I worried over in this writing? Who *is* my audience? Todavía soy la hija de mi mamá. Keep thinking, *it's the daughters*. It's the daughters who remain loyal to the mother. She is the only woman we stand by. It is not always reciprocated. To be free means on some level to cut that painful loyalty when it begins to punish us. Stop the chain of events. La procesión de mujeres, sufriendo. Dolores my grandmother, Dolores her daughter, Dolores her daughter's daughter. Free the daughter to love her own daughter. It is the daughters who are my audience.

I write this on the deathbed of my abuela. We have made one last procession to her. My mother, my sister, her daughter and I. My grandmother's eyes are open today. I hold the bone of her skull in the palm of my hand. It is a light bird-weight.

I whisper in her better ear. "¿Abuelita? ¿Me Reconoce? Soy Cherríe, grandma. Acabo de llegar de Nueva York."

"¡Ay, Chorizo!"* She recognizes me. "Mi'jita!" Pulling my head into the deep bowl of her thin neck, she kisses me. " Mi chorizito! ¡Tengo hambre! ¡Quiero Chorizo! ¡Tengo tanta hambre!" She kids as she used to and as always I give her the fleshy part of my arm for her to mimick taking a bite from it.

"¿Donde 'stá tu mamá?" she wants to know.

"Aquí 'stoy, mamá." My mother grabs her hand.

"Elvira ¿Y La JoAnn, 'stá quí también?"

"Sí grandma, aquí 'stoy y Erin," my sister says lifting her daughter up to give my abuela a kiss.

"Hi little grandma," Erin says softly.

"¡Ay, mi chulita!" She wraps her thin veined hands around Erin's cheeks, then gnashes her teeth together, shaking her head, pretending like she wants to eat her up. It seems to me that

---

* Literally, a Mexican sausage. A nickname my grandmother has for me.

my abuelita has never been so full of life.

I am holding the moment. La línea de las mujeres, la raíz de nuestra familia. Mi mamá tiene tanto orgullo en este momento. She has taught us well to value these simple signs of love.

I write this on the deathbed of mi abuela. On the table of a new life spread out for us to eat from.

La muerte de mi abuela. Y yo nunca le hablé en la lengua que entendiera.

THE VOICES OF THE FALLERS

Because Jay Freeman was imprisoned at the age of nineteen for over twenty years because she murdered the son of her lesbian lover by throwing him off a cliff. And, because, at the age of nineteen, my high school friend Charlotte, also a lesbian, fell from a cliff and died.

for M.

You were born queer with the dream
of flying
from an attic with a trap
door   opening
to a girl who could
handle a white horse
with wings   riding her
away   opening
to a girl who could
save a woman
on a white horse
riding her
away.

I was born queer with the dream
of falling
the small sack of my body
dropping
off a ledge
suddenly.

> *Listen.*
> Can you hear my mouth crack
> open   the sound

1

of my lips bending
back against the force
of the fall?

Listen.
Put your ear deep
down
through   the opening
of my throat and
listen.

...

The nun said
"Young lady
you have a chip
on your shoulder
that's going to get you
in plenty of trouble
some day."

The queer
flicks off
the chip
with the nonchalance
with the grace
with the cool
brush of lint
from a 200-dollar
three-piece

the chip tumbling
off
her shoulder

her   shoulder first
tumbling
off
the cliff   the legs

following
over
her head   the chip

spinning onto the classroom floor
(silently imagined)

her body's
dead

silent

collision
with the sand.

> *I'm falling*
> *can't you see*
> *I'm*
> *falling?*

...

DARE ME
DARE ME
DARE ME
to push this kid off
the cliff   DARE
ME
Some queer
mother I am
who would kill her kid
to save her own neck
from cracking
on the way down

You bet your ass I am
if push comes to shove
the kid goes
queer.

> *I'm falling*
> *can't you see*
> *I'm falling?*

...

It was not an accident

I knew then sitting in the row next to her she would not survive
she could not survive this way this unprotected defiance her
shoulders pushing up against me grabbing me by the collar up
against the locker "motherfucker you mess with my girlfriend?"

her pale face twitching
cover it up
cover it up
I wished she would
cover it up
for both our sakes
she would not
survive this way
pushing
people
around.

...

When I fell
from the cliff   she tells me
it was the purest move
I ever made   she tells me
she thought of me
as a kind of consolation
surviving
just as she made
the move
to fall
just as her shoulders split
the air.

Do you know what it feels like finally
to be up
against nothing?
Oh it's like flying, Cherríe
I'm flying

I'm falling
can't you see
I'm
falling?

   ...

She confesses to me—

I held the boy's body between my hands
for a moment it was like
making love
the bones of my fingers resting
between the bones of his ribcage
I held him there
I guess we both felt   safe
for a split   second
but then he grew
stiff and then he resisted
so I pushed
up against him
I pushed until the wall
of his body vanished
into the air so thick
it was due to eat both of us up
sooner or later.

I'm falling
can't you see
I'm
falling?
Momma, I tell you
I'm falling
right
now

   ...

In this child
killer
I could have

buried the dead
memory of Charlotte
falling   once
and for all
I could have
ended there   holding
the silence

but it is
this end
I fear.

          Waking
to the danger
of falling
again
          falling

in love   the dream.

6

*WHAT KIND OF LOVER
HAVE YOU MADE ME
MOTHER?*

IT IS YOU, MY SISTER, WHO MUST BE PROTECTED

1.

Maybe you'll understand this. My mother was not the queer one, but my father.

Something got beat out of that man. I don't know what. I don't have any stories of him much to speak of, only a memory as tame and uneventful as his movement through the house. You *do* remember the man with skin white as a baby's and that is how we thought of him—a battered child. Yeah, something hit him down so deep and so for sure, there seems to be no calling him back now.

But it is this queer I run from. This white man in me. This man settling into the pockets of a woman's vicious pride and conviction to make a life for herself and her children.

The year he was left to his own devices, we came back to find our home in shambles. My mother climbed up onto the stool in the kitchen, stuck her head into the cupboard, and started throwing onto the floor boxes and boxes of cereal, seasons-old and opened, now crawling with ants and roaches.

Do you remember that?...and how so often during those days my mom would interrogate dad, asking him about religion and god and didn't he believe *anything*. He would nod back nervously, "Sure honey sure I believe," he'd say. "I just don't know how to talk about it." And I'd stare across the top of my glass of milk and the small yellow kitchen table, and as far back as I could imagine into that wide rolling forehead, I saw nothing stirring. For the life of me, there wasn't a damn thing happening in that head of his.

It is this queer I run from. A pain that turns us to quiet surrender. No. Surrender is too active a term. There *was* no fight. Resignation.

I'm afraid of ever being that stuck. Stuck back in a story of myself as a six-year-old blond-haired boy, very quiet. I guess he was probably very quiet, even then, watching his father leave.

When dad told me the story of his father's return, the restaurant visit sixteen years later, the three hours together after a lifetime of abandonment, I asked him, "Were you angry with him, dad? How did you feel?"

"I was very nervous," he answered sighing. That's all I could get out of the man, how nervous he was.

I thought of the old man sleeping in his grave somewhere in Canada, blameless as an English saint. In our children's imagination, he was so unlike the other one, the dark one, who died a young and defiant death. We had seen that grandfather's grave with our own eyes, touched with our own hands the dry and broken earth which held the stone. I remember during those visits to Tijuana how you and I would stand so reverently at the sides of the tombstone. Our eyes following my mother carrying water in small coffee cans back and forth in silent ritual to wash the face of the grave. Then, grandma would brush it off carefully with the crumpled kleenexes she drew from her purse, until the letters of his name shown through as vividly as the man they chose to remember at that moment.

This is the portrait of a father whose memory you could live with, kicking and screaming. But the saint? I vaguely recall only one picture of my dad's dad in a double-breasted grey suit. He was standing alone. Palm trees in the background. Hat dipped.

After dad had finished the story, I sat with him watching his face slowly curl up into a squint, his eyes fluttering to a close. You know the expression—where the vertical crease along the side of his forehead deepens into a kind of scar. I realized then that he was going fast—to the place past and beyond the pain where he had laid his face in the lap of a woman and like a boy begging, promised never to ask for much, if only she would keep him there.

I wanted to shake the man from his grave! Bring him back to life for a reckoning! But it's hard, I'm sure you feel this too, to sustain any passion, really, for my father.

Daddy, you did not beat me, but every blow I took
from the hand of my mother came from a caress
you could not give her.

*The hole burning through her belly had nothing to do
with my lack of loving. I loved her through and through,
alive and in the flesh.*

*We women settle for dead men with cold or absent touches.
We carry the weight of your deaths, and yet we bore you
as the first life you knew.*

*You have your father to thank, father, for his leaving you.
Not your mother nor mine who fed you all the days of your life.*

2.

The only time I ever saw my father cry, sober, was about six
months after his mother's death. Do you remember? We must've
been only about five and six and we had gone to see a movie, a
famous one, I don't recall the name. But a woman dies at the end
in a hospital bed. And my dad, later, driving the family home,
suddenly out of nowhere begins to cry. I don't, at first, under-
stand that he is crying, only that he is making these strange
blurting noises, his head falling down onto his chest. Then I hear
my mom in the front seat snap, "Pull over, Jim! Pull over!" Like
she were talking to a child. And my dad does. Draping his arms
over the steering wheel, he starts bawling like a baby.

There seemed to be no tears. I don't remember seeing any. I
only knew that I had never seen a person, a grown man, look so
out of his body. Lost. Awkward. Trying to reach for a cry so
much deeper than the one he was hitting on.

3.

My mother tells me that it is you, my sister, who must be
protected. That this will hurt you too much. But I can under-
stand these things. I am worldly and full of knowledge when
something goes queer.

Splitting a beer between us, she says, "Cecilia, mi'jita, your
father, he has no feeling left in him." I think, *this is no news.* "It's
in a certain place in his body," she explains. The absence.

She asks me, have I noticed how he's "so soft, not very
manly?"

10

"Yeah, mamá, I've noticed," I say too eagerly, hungry for the first time to speak of my father with *some* kind of compassion. A real feeling.
"I think he's different like you, ¿entiendes? Pero, no digas nada a tu hermana."
"No, mamá," I say, "but daddy seems to love men. It's true. You know how he always gets so excited with any ole new friend he makes at the plant. Like a kid. How he goes overboard when my brother or cousins are around. Not like the way he is around women, just part of the scenery." I regret these last words, seeing her face flinch.
I bite my tongue down hard, holding it. I must not say too much. I must not know too much. But I am so excited, thinking of the possibility of my father awakened to the touch. Imagining my father feeling *something* deep and profound and alive.

Alive.

She knows the difference, she says, she knows what it's like to have a "real" man touch her. "If it hadn't been for Baker, the first one, she says, maybe I wouldn't of known, maybe it wouldn't of mattered, but...forty years mi'jita, forty years."
Grabbing my hand across the table, "Honey, I know what it's like to be touched by a man who wants a woman. I don't feel this with your father," squeezing me. "¿Entiendes?"
The room falls silent then as if the walls, themselves, begged for a moment to swallow back the secret that had just leaked out from them. And it takes every muscle in me, *not* to leave my chair, *not* to climb through the silence, *not* to clamber toward her, *not* to touch her the way I know she wants to be touched.
"Yeah, Mamá, I understand."
Pulling her hand back, she pours the last few drops left in the bottle into my glass. "Talk to your father," she says. "He listens to you. Don't let him know you know. Tiene vergüenza."

The ride back to the airport.

I am driving his car. Feeling more man than my father. The car is entrusted to me to handle. I am on a mission. I am man enough to handle the situation, having a sex-talk with my father.

But I can't say anything decent to the man; I'm not supposed to know. I must only be a son to him, supportive, encouraging, reliable—stroking and coaxing the subject.

How to advise a man and keep his manliness intact?

"Daddy?"

"Uh-huh?"

"Sometimes when you've gotten hurt, you know, and..."

"Uh-huh."

"...you...you can't let yourself feel it..."

"Uh-huh...," nodding.

"...like you feel..."

"Uh-huh."

"...dead all over."

"Uh-huh...," nodding. "Uh-huh," nodding.

"It can catch up with you..."

"Uh-huh...sure, honey. Uh-huh."

"...and you start..."

"Uh-huh."

"...forgetting how..."

"Uh-huh...," nodding.

"...to feel."

"Uh-huh." Bobbing.

"You need to let your feelings out more..."

"Uh-huh."

"...Dad."

"Sure, honey." Nodding.

Bobbing.

Beating.

"I see..."

a

dead

"...what you mean."

horse.

"Mom's worried about you, Dad," wrapping the conversation up as I wrap around the last interchange.
"Yep. I'll sure try to be better to your mother," he says.

At the airport, we have a drink together. Right there on the shoulders of my sensitivity. If I were a man, I could be one bastard of a sensitive guy. Since I am a woman, people—men and women alike—drink from me. I am the eternal well of pathos.

When is someone going to make love to *me*, unequivocally. Me. I am worried about me. mother sister brother father. All of you. Boarding the plane, I want to say, *Daddy, I am worried about me.*

From my window, I can see him now behind the grill of the fence. He'll go home thinking we had a good conversation, scratching at something. It tingles of *something* alive, breathing still. A small pale man waiting like a father, like...

The plane begins to roll.

beating a dead horse, I think.

When is someone going to make love to *me*, unequivocally?

LA DULCE CULPA

What kind of lover have you made me, mother
who drew me into bed with you at six/at sixteen
oh, even at sixty-six you do still
lifting up the blanket with one arm
lining out the space for my body with the other

    as if our bodies still beat
    inside the same skin
    as if you never noticed
    when they cut me
    out
    from you.

What kind of lover have you made me, mother
who took belts to wipe this memory from me

    the memory of your passion
    dark & starving, spilling
    out of rooms, driving
    into my skin, cracking
    & cussing in spanish

    the think dark *f* sounds
    hard *c's* splitting
    the air like blows

    you would *get a rise out of me*
    you knew it in our blood
    the vision   of my rebellion

What kind of lover have you made me, mother
who put your passion on a plate for me
nearly digestible. Still trying to swallow
the fact that we lived most of our lives

with the death of a man
whose touch ran
across the surface of your skin
never landing nightly
where you begged it
to fall

　　　to hold your desire
　　　in the palm of his hand

　　　for you to rest there
　　　for you to continue.

What kind of lover have you made me, mother
so in love

with what is left

unrequited.

WHAT IS LEFT

Mamá
I use you
like the belt
pressed inside your grip
seething for contact

I take
what I know
from you and want
to whip this world
into shape
            the damage
has defined me
as the space you provide
for me in your bed

...

I was not to raise an arm against you

But today
I promise you
I *will* fight back

Strip the belt from your hands

and take you

into
my arms.

LIKE FAMILY

Loving on the Run

THE PILGRIMAGE

She saw women
maybe the first time
when they had streamed in long broken
single file
out from her mother's tongue—

    "En México, las mujeres crawl
    on their hands and knees
    to the basilica door.
    This proves their faith."

The brown knotted knees were hers
in her dreaming, she wondered
where in the journey
would the dusty knees begin
to crack,
    would the red blood of the women
    stain the grey bone of the road.

LATER, SHE MET JOYCE

1

Later, she met Joyce
and after they had been friends for a whole
school year, formed their own
girls' gang with code words & rhymes
that played itself cooly
on *this* side of trouble
they got separated by the summer.

Joyce, without a phone
and so far away
into the bordering
town.

But just once, they rendezvoused
on the front porch of a pair
of old white folks, friends of the family.
"Come see me," Joyce whispered
over the telephone line. "I'm
only a few blocks away."

And without expecting to, Cecilia climbed
right up those steps and straight into Joyce's
arms and she would never forget the shape
of the girl's chest, a good one
and a half year's older and
how her own small chest & cheek
sunk into it.
It spread through her body
the cool breath and release
of a tightness she didn't know
she had held back, waiting
for the summer's end.
Waiting to look
into Joyce's round-like-an-olive
face and see it, full of tears, too.

It was the first time for both of them.

And Cecilia thought, *so this is love.*

2

Later, she met Joyce
who didn't come back
to cath-lic school
it being too hard she guessed
(there *was* no telephone)
in a big winter coat
after mass one sunday
looking more like a momma
than her childhood friend.
Rounder than Cecilia had ever seen her
hair teased high off her head.

"Hi." Cecilia said.
"Eh, ésa, 'ow you doing? Whadchu say, man?"

Joyce moved back and forth, her suedes
toeing the ground, talking that talk
that Cecilia's momma called
a difernt claz o' people
that had something to do with your tongue
going thick on you, wearing
shiny clothes and never getting
to college.

Seems in other people's eyes
Joyce was a fat half-breed
that flunked close-to-twice
in other people's eyes
in other people's eyes.

In Joyce's eyes that morning
Cecilia looked for a sign,

*C'mon Joyce   be kidding   please
you remember me   you remember
me   you remember
please*

and thought she detected
some trace there between the two thick lines
of torquoise, of the brown eyes that cried
over missing her.

Missing Joyce turned
pachuca on her, walking away
talking about the "guyz"
she would like to have
ride her low
through the valley floor.

3
Later that year,
Cecilia was picked
by the smart
white
girls
for president.

AN OPEN INVITATION TO A MEAL

I am
you tell me
a piece of cake.

I wonder about your eating habits
which make me dessert
instead of staple
a delicacy, like some chocolate mousse
teasing your taste buds, melting
in your mouth—stopping there.

There's nothing pretty about me.

I am brown and grainy and can stick to the ribs
a food source that won't run out on you
through the toughest winter.

Come, sit down.
Give up that sweet tooth
and we'll put in a jar
to remind us of the polite
society that can afford
such things.

Right now, it's beginning to snow.

Come, sit down. The day is
getting shorter and it's beginning
to snow.

Yes, here.

Sit down.

Here.

YOU UPSET THE WHOLE SYSTEM OF THIS PLACE

for Julie

I've been inside all day.

you enter sleek, wet from winter rain. hot heaving chest. hot breath. the still heatered air of this house melts around your shoulders as you pass through it, dripping down along your thighs to bare calloused feet. you upset the whole system of this place.

approaching, your footsteps are solid and silent.

I, wrapped in bedclothes, billows of quilts and pillows. I rock to the rhythmic sound of my own breathing inside my head. stuffed mucus. my small chest, a battleground. it is fragile and bony. a cough that scrapes it dry each time. an ache like a rash beneath my ribs.

all that keeps you from me is this guatemalan drape which lines my bed like a mosquito net, only one simple striped panel. you wave it aside with a backhand motion. you move into the bed with me, not afraid of catching cold. the thick warm dough of your hand pours into the hollow parts of me.

"I've been trying not to cry for you all day," I say. You stroke my mouth closed.
"I need you now, I have this terrible cold."

without reply, you go into the green kitchen and pull out the remains of a gallon of cider. I imagine you crushing the nutmeg into the liquid while it warms over the low flame, squeezing in lemon, imitating me.

you return, mug in hand. you are dry now. your hair straggly. I drink the hot cider and you stay and roll with me until dinnertime. you ease me a half an hour into the night.

"Are you coming back?"

"Yes," you answer, "when you're better."

then I lean into your cheek, breathing in with my mouth.

I follow your footsteps exiting through the hardwood hallway, down a step, across the carpet, out the door, and down the many red wet steps into the night that swallows you up.

LOVING ON THE RUN

for women who travel in packs of one

1
I found you on a street corner
hangin out with a bunch of boys
lean brown boys
you too lean
into them
talkin your girl-head off
with your glasses
like some wizard
sayin
"I know what that feels like."

I found you there
you guys hangin out
like family to each other
talkin about women
you sayin
how they make your hips roll
without thinkin
those pale green
hips of yours
deep and oiled
like a woman

they don't catch on
about you bein one
for all your talk about women/likin them
they don't catch the difference
for all your talk about
your common enemy
you operatin on a street sense
so keen that it can spot danger

25

before he makes it around the corner
before he scarcely notices you
as a woman
they marvel at this

they don't catch on
them seein your words
like the body of a dark brother
you sayin
"I know what that feels like"
being shitted on
and they believin you
about your allied place on the block
about the war goin on
they believin you
because you know
you got
no reason
to lie to them

2
I found you among blarin stereos
while walkin thru the neighborhood
there you were
kicked back on some porch
actin like family
like you belonged
callin to me
hangin over the railing
wavin
coaxin me to your steps
gettin me to sit there
you strokin my head
slow and soft, sayin
"you are soooo sweet"
drawin out the "so"
like a long drink
like a deep moan

comin out from inside you
like a deep sigh
of lovin

lovin
like your brothers
lovin hard-won
lovin gotten in snatches
in collisions
in *very* desperate situations
lovin which sometimes squatted
rested
took a vacation
would not get up off its ass
to meet a woman
face on
lovin on the run

3

collecting me
into your thin arms
you are woman to me
and brother to them
in the same breath
you marvel at this

seeing yourself
for the first time
in the body of this sister
like family
like you belong
you moving up against this woman
like you this streetfighter
like you whom
you've taken in
under your bruised wing
your shoulderblade bent
on bearing alone

seeing yourself
for the *first* time
in the body of her boyhood
her passion to survive
female and *un*compromising

taking all this under your wing
letting it wrestle there
into your skin
       changing you

LOVING IN THE WAR YEARS

Loving you is like living
in the war years.
I *do* think of Bogart & Bergman
not clear who's who
but still singin a long smoky
mood into the piano bar
drinks straight up
the last bottle in the house
while bombs split
outside, a broken
world.

A world war going on
but you and I still insisting
in each our own heads
still thinkin how
if I could only make some contact
with that woman across the keyboard
we size each other up
        yes...

Loving you has this kind of desperation
to it, like do or die, I
having eyed you from the first
time you made the decision to move
from your stool
to live dangerously.

All on the hunch
that in our exchange of photos
of old girlfriends, names
of cities and memories
back in the states
the fronts we've manned
out here on the continent
all this on the hunch

that *this* time there'll be
no need for resistance.

Loving in the war years
calls for this kind of risking
without a home to call our own
I've got to take you as you come
to me, each time like a stranger
all over again. Not knowing
what deaths you saw today
I've got to take you
as you come, battle bruised
refusing our enemy, fear.

We're all we've got. You and I

maintaining
this war time morality
where being queer
and female is as rude
as we can get.

THE SLOW DANCE

Thinking of Elena, Susan—watching them dance together. The images return to me, hold me, stir me, prompt me to want *something*.

Elena moving Susan around the floor, so in control of the knowledge: how to handle this woman, while I fumble around them. When Elena and I kissed, just once, I forgot and let too much want show, closing my eyes, all the eyes around me seeing me close my eyes. I am a girl wanting so much to kiss a woman. She sees this too, cutting the kiss short.

But not with Susan, Susan's arm around Elena's neck. Elena's body all leaning into the center of her pelvis. *This is the way she enters a room*, leaning into the body of a woman.

The two of them, like grown-ups, like women. The women I silently longed for. Still, I remember after years of wanting and getting and loving, still I remember the desire to be that *in sync* with another woman's body.

And I move women around the floor, too—women I think enamored with me. My mother's words rising up from inside me—"A *real* man, when he dances with you, you'll know he's a *real* man by how he holds you in the back." I think, *yes*, someone who can guide you around a dance floor and so, I do. Moving these women kindly, surely, even superior. *I can handle these women*. They want this. And I do too.

Thinking of my father, how so timidly he used to take my mother onto the small square of carpet we reserved for dancing, pulling back the chairs. She really leading the step, him learning to cooperate so it *looked* like a male lead. I noticed his hand, how it lingered awkwardly about my mother's small back, his thin fingers never really getting a hold on her.

I remember this as I take a woman in my arms, my hand moving up under her shoulder blade, speaking to her from there. It is from *this* spot, the dance is directed. From *this* place, I tenderly, with each fingertip, move her.

I am my mother's lover. The partner she's been waiting for. I can handle whatever you got hidden. I can provide for you.

But when I put this provider up against the likes of Elena, *I* am the one following/falling into her. Like Susan, taken up in the arms of this woman. *I want this.*

Catching the music shift; the beat softens, slows down. I search for Elena—the bodies, the faces. *I am ready for you now.* I want age. knowledge. *Your body that still, after years, withholds and surrenders—keeps me there, waiting, wishing.* I push through the bodies, looking for her. Willing. Willing to feel *this time* what disrupts in me. Girl. Woman. Child. Boy. Willing to embody what I will in the space of her arms. Looking for Elena, I'm willing, wanting.

And I find you dancing with this other woman. My body both hers and yours in the flash of a glance.

I can handle this.

I am used to being an observer.
I am used to not getting what I want.
I am used to imagining what it must be like.

FEAR, A LOVE POEM

1

If fear is two girls awakening in the same room
after a lifetime of sleeping together
she saying, *I dreamed it was the end of the world
sister, it was the end*   you knowing this in your sleep
her terror seeping through skin into your dreams, holding her
sensing something moving too fast

> as with a lover,
> dressing and dreaming
> in the same room.

If fear is awakening in the same room
feeling something moving too fast
the body next to you awake   the back ignoring
your dream which breaks *her* sleep, too   you
waiting for the embrace to be returned   you
waiting to be met in the nightmare
by a sister, by a lover—

If fear is wishing there were some disease to call it
saying, I AM GOING CRAZY   always for lack
of a better word   always because we have no words
to say we need
attention, early on.

If fear is this, these things
then I am neither alone, nor crazy
but a child, for fear of doom, driven
to look   into the darkest
part
of the eye—

> the part of the eye
> that is not eye   at all
> but hole.

At thirteen, I had the courage
to stare that hole down   Face up
to it alone in the mirror.
I can't claim the same simple courage
now, moving away from the mirror
into the faces of other
women   to *your* face which dares
to answer mine. That it is

                    in
                    this
                    hole
                    round, common and black
                    where we recognize each other.
                    That in looking to the hole
                    the iris, with all its shades
                    of contrast and persuasion,
                    blurs peripheral
                    and I am left, standing
                    with your face
                    in my hands
                    like a mirror. This clear
                    recognition I fear
                    to see our hunger bold-faced, like this
                    sometimes turning the sockets in your head
                    stone cold, *sometimes*
                    enveloping your eyes with a liquid
                    so pure and full
                    of longing I feel
                    it could clean out the most miserable parts
                    of myself   melt down
                    a lifetime of turned backs.

          2
I know now, with you
no one's turning her back.
I may roll over and over
in my mind, toss back and forth
from shoulder   to shoulder the weight

of a child in me, battered wanting walking
through the streets   armored and ready
to kill   a body
wrestling now with the touch of your surrender
but I won't turn my back.

You reach for me in bed.
It is 4 am
your arm stretching
across a valley of killings I fear
no one can survive.
                    all this in one night, again?

you reach for me in bed
Look at me, you say, turning
my chin into your hand
what do *you see?*

It is
my face, wanting
and refusing everything.

And at that moment
for a moment, I want
to take that slender hand
and place it between my breasts
my hand holding it there.
I want to feel
your touch *outside*
my body, on the *surface*
of my skin.

I want to know, *for sure*,
where you leave off
and I begin.

PESADILLA

There came the day when Cecilia began to think about color.

Not the color of trees or painted billboards or the magnificent spreads of color laid down upon the hundreds of Victorians that lined the streets of her hometown city. She began to think about skin color. And the thought took hold of her and would not give; would not let loose. So that every person—man, woman, and child—had its particular grade of shade. And that fact meant all the difference in the world.

Soon her body began to change with this way of seeing. She felt her skin, like a casing, a beige bag into which the guts of her life were poured. And inside it, she swam through her day. Upstream. Downtown. Underground. Always, the shell of this skin, leading her around.

So that nothing seemed fair to her anymore: the war, the rent, the prices, the weather. And it spoiled her time.

Then one day, color moved in with her. Or, at least, that was how she thought of it when the going was the roughest between her and her love. That was how she thought of it after the animal had come and left. Splattered himself all around their new apartment or really the old apartment they had broken their backs to make liveable.

After brushing their way out the front door, leaving the last coat of varnish on the hard-wood floor to dry, Cecilia and Deborah had for the first time in weeks given themselves the afternoon off. They returned in the early evening, exhausted from the heat, and the crowds, and the noise of the subways and slowly began the long trek up to their sixth-floor apartment. *Why couldn't we have found an apartment with an elevator in the building,* Cecilia thought each time she found herself at the bottom of the stairs, arms full of packages, staring up at the long journey ahead of her.

But no, *this* was the apartment they had wanted—the one they believed their love could rescue from its previous incarnation.

The woman who lived there before them was said to have had five dogs and five children, crowded into the one bedroom apartment. Each time Juanito came by from across the hall to spy on them at work, he had a different version to tell of "La Loca" who had lived there before them. "She was evicted," he would announce, almost proudly, with all the authority an eight-year-old can muster, puffing out his bare brown chest. "She was so dirty, you could smell it down to the basement!"

The signs of filth, yes, still remained. But *that* Cecilia and Deborah believed they could remove—under coats of paint and plaster. The parts of broken toys found in the corners of cupboards, children's crayola markings on the wall, torn pieces of teenage magazines stuck up with dust-covered strips of scotch tape—all indicated too many people in too small a space. *¿Quién sabe la pena que sufría esa mujer?* Cecila thought.

It was the woman's rage, however, that could not be washed out of the apartment walls. There was no obliterating from Cecilia's mind the smell and sight of the dogfood she had found stuffed into the mouth of the bathroom sink—red and raw in its anger. As Cecilia scraped it out—"¡La Mierda del mundo que coma mierda!"—she tried not to believe that all this was the bad omen she suddenly felt rising hot and thick in her throat.

Finally, making it up to the sixth floor landing, the two women dropped their bags, exhausted, and Cecilia drew her keys out from her purse. But before she could turn the key in the lock, the door easily gave way. She quickly tried to convince herself that yes, she had been negligent. The last to leave. The first to forget in her fatigue to secure the lock.

But she knew different. Entering the apartment, her heart pounding, Cecilia lead the way down the long hallway—a dark labyrinth to the pesadilla that awaited them. At the end of it, she could see their bedroom, the light burning. A tornado had hit it!

No, this was not the result of some faceless natural disaster. This was a live and breathing thing. An animal. An animal had broken in.

And the women broke down. *What kind of beast* they cried *would do this?* His parts drawn all over their freshly painted walls for them to see and suck and that's what he told them there on the wall.

SUCK MY DICK   YOU HOLE

He had wanted money and finding no such thing, but a picture of a woman who could have been a sister or a lover or a momma and no sign of man around, he wrote:

I'M BLACK YOU MOTHERFUCKER BITCH
YOU BUTCH

And Cecilia knew if he had had the time and sense enough he would have even written her lover's name out there upon the bedroom wall.

He wanted Dee, too. Even in his hatred, he wanted Cecilia's lover. Everybody, it seemed, had *something* to say about Deborah's place on the planet.

Seeing his scratches on the wall, both women knew they were very close to giving it up altogether. Cecilia closing up the thought just as it broke open inside her. Closing in on Deborah, she brought the woman into her arms and they fell against the wall, crying. The animal's scrawl disappearing behind them.

It was the first time in their life together that Cecilia wondered if she were up to the task of such loving.

It had scarcely been a week since they had carried down their five flights of stairs the last torn-up suitcase of the animal's debris. They needed the rest, the relief from the city and found it in the home of friends by the Hudson, drinking iced seltzer with lime in the bake of the sun. The violation, a million miles away from the one hour's drive out of town.

Dee grew blacker as she slept on the deck. And when Cecilia rose to refill her glass it took the greatest rigidity of spine *not* to bend down and kiss the wet and shining neck of the woman stretched out before her, sound asleep.

Cecilia wanted her. She was afraid to want her.

Closing the sliding glass door behind her, the house hit Cecilia with a cool that she had nearly forgotten in the heavy humidity of the city. Even the city park could not provide this quality of coolness—cement blocks hovering around it on all fours. This was the kind of coolness that only grew from a ground now hollowed out by tunnels and steaming underground trains.

Berkeley. It reminded her of the hills of Berkeley. The blend of drying jasmine and eucalyptus hot-whipped into a cloudless sky, the scent carrying itself into the bay.

In Brooklyn, she still found it hard to believe she lived by the water. The tops of neighboring ships were to her merely another line of differently shaped structures rising up from the stiff water-floor. The real mother ocean was three thousand miles behind her.

The kitchen was flooded with sunlight and houseplants—those that hung and those that seemed to grow right out from under the linoleum floor. Cecilia found herself breathing more deeply than she had in months. She felt calmer somehow. A feeling she had left somewhere, she thought, *back in california.*

But what?...What exactly *was it?*
The smell?
The light? She held the bottle to pour. *Yes, both these things, but...*
"Salud." She mimed a toast in the air, pushing back the thought coming at her, her heart speeding up.

It was...white.
It was whiteness and...safety.

Old lovers that carried their whiteness like freedom/and breath/ and light. Their shoulders, always straight-backed and sweetly oiled for color. In their faces, the luxury of trust.

It was whiteness and money.

In this way, she had learned to be a lesbian. Not that any of her friends actually had cash on hand. In fact, she was the one among them who came from the least, but who always seemed to have the most—the one that always managed to find something "steady." But there was the ambience of money: the trips cross-country, the constant career changes, the pure cotton clothing, and yes, the sunshine. In her memory, it was never dark, except at night when it was always quiet and nearly suburban.

But the feeling she remembered most, the feeling that she could not shake, was of some other presence living amongst them. Some white man somewhere—their names always mono-syllabled: Tom, Dick, Jack. Like boys, flat-topped and tough—cropping up in a photograph, a telephone call, a letter, who in the crunch, would be their ticket.

Nobody would have said that then (or even thought of it that way). Cecilia certainly wouldn't have. But she could see it now, now that they were gone—the man's threatening and benevolent presence living with them all. They were his daughters after all, as long as they remained without a man.

Blood is blood.

It was that night that Deborah had her attack (or "fit" as Deborah used to describe them, mimicking some 1930 sci-fi version of epileptics or schizophrenics). It was the first time Cecilia had ever witnessed one in Dee, although for years Dee had spoken of them, sometimes beneath a rush of tears.

Standing on her knees in bed, she would go through the motions once again of the man coming down on her with the back of his hand. The hand enlarging as it advanced—broad and blacker than she's ever seen it. "That's when my fits began," she'd say, then suddenly, "Blahblahblah-blahblah-blahblah! Po' lil cullud girl, me!"

He was the second and last man her mother kicked out.

("My babies come first." Both their mommas could have been found saying the same thing, wrists bent back into hipbones. That's what had brought them together—the dark, definite women of their childhood.)

But that night, there was no joking. Waking to Deborah's absence in the bed, Cecilia quickly got up and, entering the bathroom, found her lover thrown back against the tank of the toilet. mouth open, unconscious.

40

It was not how Cecilia had imagined it. No tongue-gagging. No gutteral sounds, no jerking movements. No joke.

Gathering the dead weight into her arms, Cecilia brought the heavy head to her chest, holding it there. The weight like a hot rock against her breastbone—the same shape of the fear now forming inside her heart.

And then, as if she had rehearsed the role, she began to rock the body. And the more she rocked, the more the motion slowly began to dissolve the stone inside her chest and allowed, finally for her tears to come. She rocked. She cried. "Oh Deborah, baby, wake up!" She cried, "¡Por Favor, despiértate! ¡Chula, por favor!" She rocked. Until at last, she felt the head stiffen and pull away.

"Get my pills," Deborah moaned.

Cecilia rushed back into the bedroom and began rumaging around in Deborah's bag, trying frantically to find the pills, finally dumping the entire contents onto the floor. There on her knees she felt something turn in her. She felt her heart like a steel clamp inside her chest, twisting what was only moments ago a living beating fear into a slow cool numbing between her breasts.

Her loving couldn't change a thing.

Cecilia remembered the first time she had ever felt this same sensation of "coldness." Her memory rushing back in flashes to the picture of a woman, her mother, elbows dug into the kitchen table, yellow, the photograph curled into her hand, yellow too, tears streaming down her cheeks.

Again. A river return.

A river whose pull always before that moment had swept Cecilia off her chair and into her mother's arms.

But on that particular day, Cecilia stepped outside the circle of pain her mother drew like hot liquid into the little girl's body. The mother's tears comingling with her own, like communion.

Cecilia didn't understand why her feelings were changing, only that they had to change. *Change or die*, she thought. And suddenly she grew stiff and fixed in her chair, hands pressed between her knees, riveted against the tide of rage and regret she knew her mother's memories would call forth. Old wounds still oozing with the blood of sinners in wartime.

41

"I forgive," her mother would announce. "But I never forget."

And mustering up what courage she could, the girl first whispered to herself, then shouted outloud, "You gotta change, Mama! You gotta let it go!"

When she didn't change. When Cecilia had prayed and pleaded, practiced and preached every form of childish support she could think of, she left the woman. It was years later, but she took a walk right out of that kitchen and family-way of passing on daughter-to-daughter misery. Her momma cursing after her, "You're just like the rest of 'em. You don't know how to love."

"Honey? Are you coming?"

"Yeah, right away, baby." Cecilia grabbed the pills and came back into the bathroom to find Deborah now with eyes open and blinking alive. But Cecilia couldn't rid herself of the feeling in her chest. It was as if a different woman had stepped back into the room and Cecilia now stood somewhere else, outside the room, watching this other one nurse her lover back to health. In silence, giving Deborah the pills. In silence, moving her back to bed. In silence, watching her fall into a deep and exhausted sleep.

Lying awake in bed, the sunlight cracking through the window, Cecilia thought of the times as a child when she always lived her nights like days while the rest of the house slept. Never soundly sleeping like the woman now curled under her arm.

Getting up six and seven times a night, locking and re-locking the doors. Praying in whispers the same prayers over and over and over again, nodding into sleep, resisting. Resisting the pictures the dreams would bring. The women, wanting. The men, like flaming devils, swollen with desire.

Locking and re-locking the doors. Keeping the fearful out, while it wrestled inside her without restraint. During those hours before dawn, *anything* was possible—the darkness giving permission for the spirit to shake itself loose in Deborah.

Cecilia wanted Dee. She was afraid to want her. Afraid to feel another woman's body. Like family.

When she discovered the first woman wouldn't change, it had sort of wrapped things up for the rest of them. Still she'd go through the changes of asking for changes como su abuelita during the english mass mouthing spanish a million miles an hour, kissing the crucifix of the rosary wrapped 'round her neck at each and every "amen."

Nothing to disturb her order of things. No matter what was said or done in english, she knew the spanish by heart. In her heart, which long ago forgot the clear young reason for the kissings, the vicious beatings of the breast, the bending to someone else's will.

What frightened Cecilia so was to feel this gradual reawakening in her bones. For weeks her hands had merely skimmed her lover's flesh, never reaching in.

Cecilia pressed her nose into Dee's hair. The sun, almost full now in the window, had warmed the fibers into a cushion of heat which promised rest, continuance. In the intake of breath, there was more familiarity, more loss of resistance, more sense of landing *somewhere* than any naming she had tried to do with words inside her head.

Words were nothing to the smell.

Pesadilla.

There is a man on the fire escape. He is crouched just below the window sill. I could barely catch the curve of his back descending, but I have seen the movement. I know it is the animal, returned.

The figure suddenly rises to attack!

D E B Ö R A H ! !

The dark woman looking in through the glass is as frightened as I am. She is weeping. I will not let her in.

43

PASSAGE

on the edge of the war near the bonfire
we taste knowledge*

there is a very old wound in me
between my legs
where I have bled, not to birth
pueblos or revolutionary
concepts or simple
sucking children

> but a memory
> of some ancient
> betrayal.

so that when you touch me
and I long to freeze, not feel
what hungry longing I used to know
nor taste in you a want
I fear will burn
my fingers to their roots
> *it's out of my control.*

you mouth opens, I long for dryness.
The desert, untouched.
Sands swept without sweat.

Aztlan.**

---

* NOTHING IN THE WORD, *Versions of Aztec Poetry.* Stephen Berg.
(New York: Grossman Publishers, 1972).

** The mythical/historical place, in the area of present-day northern
New Mexico, from where the Aztecs were to have migrated before
settling in what is now Mexico City. It is the mythical homeland of the
present-day Chicano people.

Pero, es un sueño. This safety
of the desert.
My country was not like that.
        Neither was yours.

We have always bled
with our veins
and legs
open
to forces
beyond our control.

VIEW OF THREE
BRIDGES

RAW EXPERIENCE

1

There is this motor inside me
propelling me
forward

I watch myself for clues.

The hands in front of me
conducting me through this house
a spoon too soon wiped clean
the hands sweeping it away
barely experiencing
the sensation of fullness
usefulness

I watch myself for clues.

Catch my face, a moving portrait
in a storefront window
am taken aback
by the drop
in cheekline
my face sinking into itself

I watch myself for clues.

Say "extricate"
for the first time in my life
feel the sound
bulldoze out of my mouth

    I earned that word somewhere
    the syllables secretly meeting within me
    planning to blast me open.

There *is* this motor inside me
propelling me
forward.

I watch myself for clues,
trying to catch up
inhabit my body
again.

2

On the highest point of a hill
sitting, there is
the view of three bridges

each one with a special feature

a color
an island
a view of the red rock

Each with a particular destination
coming and going.

I watch them for clues

their secrets
about making connections
about getting
someplace.

LA GÜERA

*It requires something more than personal experience to gain a
philosophy or point of view from any specific event. It is the
quality of our response to the event and our capacity to enter into
the lives of others that help us to make their lives and experiences
our own.*

—Emma Goldman*

I am the very well-educated daughter of a woman who, by
the standards in this country, would be considered largely
illiterate. My mother was born in Santa Paula, Southern Cali-
fornia, at a time when much of the central valley there was still
farm land. Nearly thirty-five years later, in 1948, she was the
only daughter of six to marry an anglo, my father.

I remember all of my mother's stories, probably much better
than she realizes. She is a fine story-teller, recalling every event
of her life with the vividness of the present, noting each detail
right down to the cut and color of her dress. I remember stories of
her being pulled out of school at the ages of five, seven, nine, and
eleven to work in the fields, along with her brothers and sisters;
stories of her father drinking away whatever small profit she
was able to make for the family; of her going the long way home
to avoid meeting him on the street, staggering toward the same
destination. I remember stories of my mother lying about her age
in order to get a job as a hat-check girl at Agua Caliente
Racetrack in Tijuana. At fourteen, she was the main support of
the family. I can still see her walking home alone at 3 a.m., only
to turn all of her salary and tips over to her mother, who was
pregnant again.

The stories continue through the war years and on: walnut-
cracking factories, the Voit Rubber factory, and then the

---

* Alix Kates Shulman, "Was My Life Worth Living?" *Red Emma Speaks.*
(New York: Random House, 1972), p. 388.

computer boom. I remember my mother doing piecework for the electronics plant in our neighborhood. In the late evening, she would sit in front of the T.V. set, wrapping copper wires into the backs of circuit boards, talking about "keeping up with the younger girls." By that time she was already in her mid-fifties.

Meanwhile, I was college-prep in school. After classes, I would go with my mother to fill out job applications for her, or write checks for her at the supermarket. We would have the scenario all worked out ahead of time. My mother would sign the check before we'd get to the store. Then, as we'd approach the checkstand, she would say—within earshot of the cashier—"oh honey, you go 'head and make out the check," as if she couldn't be bothered with such an insignificant detail. No one asked any questions.

I was educated, and wore it with a keen sense of pride and satisfaction, my head propped up with the knowledge, from my mother, that my life would be easier than hers. I was educated; but more than this, I was "la güera"—fair-skinned. Born with the features of my Chicana mother, but the skin of my Anglo father, I had it made.

No one ever quite told me this (that light was right), but I knew that being light was something valued in my family (who were all Chicano, with the exception of my father). In fact, everything about my upbringing (at least what occurred on a conscious level) attempted to bleach me of what color I did have. Although my mother was fluent in it, I was never taught much Spanish at home. I picked up what I did learn from school and from over-heard snatches of conversation among my relatives and mother. She often called other lower-income Mexicans "braceros," or "wet-backs," referring to herself and family as "a different class of people." And yet, the real story was that my family, too, had been poor (some still are) and farmworkers. My mother can remember this in her blood as if it were yesterday. But this is something she would like to forget (and rightfully), for to her, on a basic economic level, being Chicana meant being "less." It was through my mother's desire to protect her children from poverty and illiteracy that we became "anglocized"; the more effectively we could pass in the white world, the better guaranteed our future.

From all of this, I experience, daily, a huge disparity between what I was born into and what I was to grow up to become. Because, (as Goldman suggests) these stories my mother told me crept under my "güera" skin. I had no choice but to enter into the life of my mother. *I had no choice*. I took her life into my heart, but managed to keep a lid on it as long as I feigned being the happy, upwardly mobile heterosexual.

When I finally lifted the lid to my lesbianism, a profound connection with my mother reawakened in me. It wasn't until I acknowledged and confronted my own lesbianism in the flesh, that my heartfelt identification with and empathy for my mother's oppression—due to being poor, uneducated, and Chicana—was realized. My lesbianism is the avenue through which I have learned the most about silence and oppression, and it continues to be the most tactile reminder to me that we are not free human beings.

You see, one follows the other. I had known for years that I was a lesbian, had felt it in my bones, had ached with the knowledge, gone crazed with the knowledge, wallowed in the silence of it. Silence *is* like starvation. Don't be fooled. It's nothing short of that, and felt most sharply when one has had a full belly most of her life. When we are not physically starving, we have the luxury to realize psychic and emotional starvation. It is from this starvation that other starvations can be recognized—if one is willing to take the risk of making the connection—if one is willing to be responsible to the result of the connection. For me, the connection is an inevitable one.

What I am saying is that the joys of looking like a white girl ain't so great since I realized I could be beaten on the street for being a dyke. If my sister's being beaten because she's Black, it's pretty much the same principle. We're both getting beaten any way you look at it. The connection is blatant; and in the case of my own family, the difference in the privileges attached to looking white instead of brown are merely a generation apart.

In this country, lesbianism is a poverty—as is being brown, as is being a woman, as is being just plain poor. The danger lies in ranking the oppressions. *The danger lies in failing to acknowledge the specificity of the oppression.* The danger lies in attempting to deal with oppression purely from a theoretical base. Without an emotional, heartfelt grappling with the source of our own oppression, without naming the enemy within ourselves and outside of us, no authentic, non-hierarchical connection among oppressed groups can take place.

When the going gets rough, will we abandon our so-called comrades in a flurry of racist/heterosexist/what-have-you panic? To whose camp, then, should the lesbian of color retreat? Her very presence violates the ranking and abstraction of oppression. Do we merely live hand to mouth? Do we merely struggle with the "ism" that's sitting on top of our heads?

The answer is: yes, I think first we do; and we must do so thoroughly and deeply. But to fail to move out from there will only isolate us in our own oppression—will only insulate, rather than radicalize us.

To illustrate: a gay white male friend of mine once confided to me that he continued to feel that, on some level, I didn't trust him because he was male; that he felt, really, if it ever came down to a "battle of the sexes," I might kill him. I admitted that I might very well. He wanted to understand the source of my distrust. I responded, "You're not a woman. Be a woman for a day. Imagine being a woman." He confessed that the thought terrified him because, to him, being a woman meant being raped by men. He *had* felt raped by men; he wanted to forget what that meant. What grew from that discussion was the realization that in order for him to create an authentic alliance with me, he must deal with the primary source of his own sense of oppression. He must, first, emotionally come to terms with what it feels like to be a victim. If he—or anyone—were to truly do this, it would be impossible to discount the oppression of others, except by again forgetting how we have been hurt.

And yet, oppressed groups are forgetting all the time. There are instances of this in the rising Black middle class, and certainly an obvious trend of such "capitalist-unconsciousness" among white gay men. Because to remember may mean giving up whatever privileges we have managed to squeeze out of this society by virtue of our gender, race, class, or sexuality.

Within the women's movement, the connections among women of different backgrounds and sexual orientations have been fragile, at best. I think this phenomenon is indicative of our failure to seriously address ourselves to some very frightening questions: How have I internalized my own oppression? How have I oppressed? Instead, we have let rhetoric do the job of poetry. Even the word "oppression" has lost its power. We need a new language, better words that can more closely describe women's fear of and resistance to one another; words that will not always come out sounding like dogma.

What prompted me in the first place to work on an anthology by radical women of color* was a deep sense that I had a valuable insight to contribute, by virtue of my birthright and my background. And yet, I don't really understand first-hand what it feels like being shitted on for being brown. I understand much more about the joys of it—being Chicana and having family are synonymous for me. What I know about loving, singing, crying, telling stories, speaking with my heart and hands, even having a sense of my own soul comes from the love of my mother, aunts, cousins...

But at the age of twenty-seven, it is frightening to acknowledge that I have internalized a racism and classism, where the object of oppression is not only someone *outside* my skin, but the someone *inside* my skin. In fact, to a large degree, the real battle with such oppression, for all of us, begins under the skin. I have had to confront the fact that much of what I value about being Chicana, about my family, has been subverted by anglo culture and my own cooperation with it. This realization did not occur to me overnight. For example, it wasn't until long after my graduation from the private college I'd attended in Los Angeles, that I realized the major reason for my total alienation from and fear of my classmates was rooted in class and culture.

Three years after graduation, in an apple-orchard in Sonoma, a friend of mine (who comes from an Italian Irish working-class family) says to me, "Cherríe, no wonder you felt like such a nut in school. Most of the people there were white and rich." It was true. All along I had felt the difference, but not until I had put the words "class" and "race" to the experience, did my

* "La Güera" was originally written for and appeared in *This Bridge Called My Back: Writings by Radical Women of Color*, an anthology co-edited with Gloria Anzaldua. (Boston: Persephone Press, 1981).

feelings make any sense. For years, I had berated myself for not being as "free" as my classmates. I completely bought that they simply had more guts than I did—to rebel against their parents and run around the country hitch-hiking, reading books and studying "art." They had enough privilege to be atheists, for chrissake. There was no one around filling in the disparity for me between their parents, who were Hollywood filmmakers, and my parents, who wouldn't know the name of a filmmaker if their lives depended on it (and precisely because their lives didn't depend on it, they couldn't be bothered). But I knew nothing about "privilege" then. White was right. Period. I could pass. If I got educated enough, there would never be no telling.

Three years after that, I had a similar revelation. In a letter to a friend, I wrote:

> I went to a concert where Ntosake Shange was reading. There, everything exploded for me. She was speaking in a language that I knew—in the deepest parts of me—existed, and that I ignored in my own feminist studies and even in my own writing. What Ntosake caught in me is the realization that in my development as a poet, I have, in many ways, denied the voice of my own brown mother—the brown in me. I have acclimated to the sound of a white language which, as my father represents it, does not speak to the emotions in my poems—emotions which stem from the love of my mother.
>
> The reading was agitating. Made me uncomfortable. Threw me into a week-long terror of how deeply I was affected. I felt that I had to start all over again. That I turned only to the perceptions of white middle-class women to speak for me and all women. I am shocked by my own ignorance.

Sitting in that auditorium chair was the first time I had realized to the core of me that for years I had disowned the language I knew best—ignored the words and rhythms that were the closest to me. The sounds of my mother and aunts gossiping—half in English, half in Spanish—while drinking cerveza in the kitchen. And the hands—I had cut off the hands in my poems. But not in conversation; still the hands could not be kept down. Still they insisted on moving.

The reading had forced me to remember that I knew things from my roots. But to remember puts me up against what I don't know. Shange's reading agitated me because she spoke with power about a world that is both alien and common to me: "the capacity to enter into the lives of others." But you can't just take the goods and run. I knew that then, sitting in the Oakland auditorium (as I know in my poetry), that the only thing worth writing about is what seems to be unknown and, therefore, fearful.

The "unknown" is often depicted in racist literature as the "darkness" within a person. Similarly, sexist writers will refer to fear in the form of the vagina, calling it "the orifice of death." In contrast, it is a pleasure to read works such as Maxine Hong Kingston's *Woman Warrior*, where fear and alienation are depicted as "the white ghosts." And yet, the bulk of literature in this country reinforces the myth that what is dark and female is evil. Consequently, each of us—whether dark, female, or both— has in some way *internalized* this oppressive imagery. What the oppressor often succeeds in doing is simply *externalizing* his fears, projecting them into the bodies of women, Asians, gays, disabled folks, whoever seems most "other."

> call me
> roach and presumptuous
> nightmare on your white pillow
> your itch to destroy
> the indestructible
> part of yourself

—Audre Lorde*

But it is not really difference the oppressor fears so much as similarity. He fears he will discover in himself the same aches, the same longings as those of the people he has shitted on. He fears the immobilization threatened by his own incipient guilt.

* From "The Brown Menace or Poem to the Survival of Roaches," *The New York Head Shop and Museum* (Detroit: Broadside, 1974), p. 48.

He fears he will have to change his life once he has seen himself in the bodies of the people he has called different. He fears the hatred, anger, and vengeance of those he has hurt.

This is the oppressor's nightmare, but it is not exclusive to him. We women have a similar nightmare, for each of us in some way has been both oppressed and the oppressor. We are afraid to look at how we have failed each other. We are afraid to see how we have taken the values of our oppressor into our hearts and turned them against ourselves and one another. We are afraid to admit how deeply "the man's" words have been ingrained in us.

To assess the damage is a dangerous act. I think of how, even as a feminist lesbian, I have so wanted to ignore my own homophobia, my own hatred of myself for being queer. I have not wanted to admit that my deepest personal sense of myself has not quite "caught up" with my "woman-identified" politics. I have been afraid to criticize lesbian writers who choose to "skip over" these issues in the name of feminism. In 1979, we talk of "old gay" and "butch and femme" roles as if they were ancient history. We toss them aside as merely patriarchal notions. And yet, the truth of the matter is that I have sometimes taken society's fear and hatred of lesbians to bed with me. I have sometimes hated my lover for loving me. I have sometimes felt "not women enough" for her. I have sometimes felt "not man enough." For a lesbian trying to survive in a heterosexist society, there is no easy way around these emotions. Similarly, in a white-dominated world, there is little getting around racism and our own internalization of it. It's always there, embodied in someone we least expect to rub up against.

When we do rub up against this person, *there* then is the challenge. *There* then is the opportunity to look at the nightmare within us. But we usually shrink from such a challenge.

Time and time again, I have observed that the usual response among white women's groups when the "racism issue" comes up is to deny the difference. I have heard comments like, "Well, we're open to *all* women; why don't they (women of color) come? You can only do so much..." But there is seldom any analysis of how the very nature and structure of the group itself may be founded on racist or classist assumptions. More importantly, so often the women seem to feel no loss, no lack, no absence when women of color are not involved; therefore, there is little desire to change the situation. This has hurt me deeply. I have come to believe that the only reason women of a privileged class will dare to look at *how* it is that *they* oppress, is when they've come to know the meaning of their own oppression. And understand that the oppression of others hurts them personally.

The other side of the story is that women of color and white working-class women often shrink from challenging white middle-class women. It is much easier to rank oppressions and set up a hierarchy, rather than take responsibility for changing our own lives. We have failed to demand that white women, particularly those that claim to be speaking for all women, be accountable for their racism.

The dialogue has simply not gone deep enough.

In conclusion, I have had to look critically at my claim to color, at a time when, among white feminist ranks, it is a "politically correct" (and sometimes peripherally advantageous) assertion to make. I must acknowledge the fact that, physically, I have had a *choice* about making that claim, in contrast to women who have not had such a choice, and have been abused for their color. I must reckon with the fact that for most of my life, by virtue of the very fact that I am white-looking, I identified with and aspired toward white values, and that I rode the wave of that Southern California privilege as far as conscience would let me.

Well, now I feel both bleached and beached. I feel angry about this—the years when I refused to recognize privilege, both when it worked against me, and when I worked it, ignorantly, at the expense of others. These are not settled issues. This is why this work feels so risky to me. It continues to be discovery. It has brought me into contact with women who invariably know a hell of a lot more than I do about racism, as experienced in the flesh, as revealed in the flesh of their writing.

I think: what is my responsibility to my roots: both white and brown, Spanish-speaking and English? I am a woman with a foot in both worlds. I refuse the split. I feel the necessity for dialogue. Sometimes I feel it urgently.

But one voice is not enough, nor two, although this is where dialogue begins. It is essential that feminists confront their fear of and resistance to each other, because without this, there *will* be no bread on the table. Simply, we will not survive. If we could make this connection in our heart of hearts, that if we are serious about a revolution—better—if we seriously believe there should be joy in our lives (real joy, not just "good times"), then we need one another. We women need each other. Because my/your solitary, self-asserting "go-for-the-throat-of-fear" power is not enough. The real power, as you and I well know, is collective. I can't afford to be afraid of you, nor you of me. If it takes head-on collisions, let's do it. This polite timidity is killing us.

As Lorde suggests in the passage I cited earlier, it is looking to the nightmare that the dream is found. There, the survivor emerges to insist on a future, a vision, yes, born out of what is dark and female. The feminist movement must be a movement of such survivors, a movement with a future.

September 1979

FOR THE COLOR OF MY MOTHER

I am a white girl gone brown to the blood color of my mother
speaking to her through the unnamed part of the mouth
the wide-arched muzzle of brown women

at two
my upper lip split open
clear to the tip of my nose
it spilled forth a cry that would not yield
that travelled down six floors of hospital
where doctors wound me into white bandages
only the screaming mouth exposed

the gash sewn back into a snarl
would last for years

I am a white girl gone brown to the blood color of my mother
speaking for her

at five, *her* mouth
pressed into a seam
a fine blue child's line drawn across her face
her mouth, pressed into mouthing english
mouthing yes yes yes
mouthing stoop lift carry
(sweating wet sighs into the field
her red bandana comes loose from under the huge brimmed hat
moving across her upper lip)

at fourteen, her mouth
painted, the ends drawn up
the mole in the corner colored in darker larger mouthing yes
she praying no no no
lips pursed and moving

at forty-five, her mouth
bleeding into her stomach

the hole gaping growing redder
deepening with my father's pallor
finally stitched shut from hip to breastbone
    an inverted V
    Vera
    Elvira

I am a white girl gone brown to the blood color of my mother
speaking for her

as it should be,
dark women come to me
               sitting in circles
I pass thru their hands
the head of my mother
painted in clay colors

      touching each carved feature swollen eyes and mouth

they understand the explosion, the splitting
open   contained within the fixed expression

they cradle her silence

          nodding to me

IT'S THE POVERTY

for Kim

You say to me,
"Take a drive with me
up the coast, babe
and bring your typewriter."

All the way down the coast
you and she stopped at motels
your typewriters tucked under your free arm
dodging the rain fast to the shelter
of metal awnings, red and white
I imagine them—you two
snorting brandy in those vinyl rooms
propping your each machine onto an end table.

  ...

This story becomes you.
A fiction I invent with my ears
evoking heroism in the first
description of the weather.

I say
my typewriter sticks in the wet.
I have been using the same ribbon
over and over and over again.
Yes, we both agree I could use
a new ribbon. But it's the poverty
the poverty of my imagination, we agree.
I lack imagination you say.

No. I lack language.

The language to clarify
my resistance to the literate.

Words are a war to me.
They threaten my family.

To gain the word to describe the loss,
I risk losing everything.
I may create a monster,
the word's length and body
swelling up colorful and thrilling
looming over my *mother*, characterized.
Her voice in the distance
unintelligible   illiterate.

These are the monster's words.

    ...

Understand.
My family is poor.
Poor. I can't afford
a new ribbon. The risk
of this one
is enough
to keep me moving
through it, accountable.
The repetition, like my mother's stories retold,
each time reveals more particulars
gains more familiarity.
You can't get me in your car so fast.

    ...

You tell me how you've learned
to write while you drive
how I can leave my droning machine behind
for all
you care.

I say, not-so-fast
not
so
fast. The drone
a chant to my ears
a common blend of histories
repeatedly inarticulate.

Not so fast.
I am poorer than you.
In my experience, fictions
are for hearing about,
not living.

WHAT DOES IT TAKE?

for Sally Gearhart upon the death of Harvey Milk

    1
The martyrs they give us
have all been men
my friend, she traces her life
through them   a series of assassinations
but not one, not
one making her bleed.

This is not the death of my mother
but my father
the kind one/the provider
pressed into newsprint
in honest good will.

If they took *you*
I would take to the streets scream, BLOODY MURDER.

But the deaths of our mothers
are never that public
they have happened before
and we were not informed.
Women do not coagulate into one
hero's death; we bleed
out of many pores, so constant
that it has come to be seen
as the way things are.

    2
Waiting
my mother's dying
was not eventful.
Expecting it

I put a hole in my arm
no TNT blast
but a slow excavation
my nails, in silent opposition
digging down to the raw part
inside the elbow.

If they took *you*
I would take to the streets
scream, BLOODY MURDER.

What does it take to move me?
your death
that I have ignored
in the deaths of other women?

Isn't the *possibility*
of your dying
enough?

SALVATION, JESUS, AND SUFFER

Last night at work, a woman younger than me with rosary beads and a scapular wrapped 'round her neck came floating into the restaurant, acting like she was gonna have a fit or something crazy—her eyelids blinking a hundred miles an hour, her eyeballs rolling up into her head, only the whites showing.

It was sunday-rush and she stood there in the middle of the floor, telling everybody they should all leave immediately because *Jesus was coming.*

And what was funny is that everybody stopped eating—their forks hanging in the air in front of their open mouths—and listened. Just for a second, but for that second, she had their complete attention.

As a nut, people noticed her. She'd be nobody if she weren't a crazy woman.

I hate religion, I said to Jeanne the hostess who kept trying to get the crazy woman to sit down, shut up, and eat some soup. I hate that she has all those words about salvation and jesus and suffer to pull off this scene with. Confusing the point.

The woman left and came back at least seven times before she finally left for good. Nobody wanted to throw her out—to where? But everytime she came in again, my stomach would get all tied up in knots and I kept getting these hits of myself at about eleven-years-old?—shaking my body up and down to rattle the "impure thoughts" outta it.

She and I—we're the same woman, but nobody notices me like that.

ANATOMY LESSON

A black woman and a small beige one talk about their bodies.
About putting a piece of their anatomy in their pockets
upon entering any given room.

When entering a room full of soldiers who fear hearts,
you put your heart in your back pocket,
the black woman explains. It is important, not to intimidate.
The soldiers wear guns, *not* in their back pockets.

You let the heart fester there. You let the heart seethe.
You let the impatience of the heart build and build
until the power of the heart hidden begins to be felt in the room.
Until the absence of the heart begins to take on the shape
of a presence.
Until the soldiers look at you and begin to beg you
to open up your heart to them, so anxious are they to see
what it is they fear they fear.

Do not be seduced.

Do not forget for a minute that the soldiers wear guns.
Hang onto your heart.
Ask them first what they'll give up to see it.
Tell them that they can begin with their arms.

Only then will *you* begin to negotiate.

IT GOT HER OVER

*"You're lucky you look the way you do, you could get any man.
Anyone says anything to you, tell them your father's white."*
　　　　—from *Claiming An Identity They Taught Me to Despise*
　　　　　　　　　　　　　　　　　Michelle Cliff

1

To touch
her skin, felt thick
like hide, not
like flesh
and blood
when an arm is raised
the blue veins shine
rivers running under-
ground with shadow
depth, and tone.

No, *her* skin
had turned on her
in the light of things.
In the light of Black
women and children
beaten/hanged/raped
strangled
murdered in Boston
Atlanta
in California where redneck
hunters coming home
with empty white hands
go off to fill 'em
with Black Man.

Her skin had turned
in the light of these things.
Stuck to her now

like a flat immovable paste
spread grey over a life.

Still,
    it got her over
in laundromats
when machines ate her change
swallowed whole her dollar bill
when cops stopped to check what the problem was
                         Remember
I could be your daughter she used
looking up from the place on the sand
where two women were spread out, defiant
where he read, *the white one*
must be protected   that time
saving them both.

It got her over
when the bill was late
when she only wanted to browse not buy
when hunger forced them
off the highway and into the grills
called "Red's" and "Friendly's"
coffee shops packed suburban
white on white, eyes shifting
to them   and away
to them   and away
and back again
then shifted into safety
lock inside their heads.

   2

She had never been ashamed of her face.

Her lust, yes
Her bad grammar, yes
Even her unforgiving ways
but never, her face
recently taken to blushing

as if the blood wanted
to swallow
        the flesh.

Bleed through
        guilt by association
        complicity to the crime.
Bleed through
        Born to lead.
        Born to love.
        Born to live.
Bleed through

and flood the joint
with a hatred so severe

people went white
with shock
and dying.

        ...

No, she had *never*
been ashamed of her face
not like this
        grabbing her own two cheeks
her fingers pressed together
as if to hold between them
the thin depth of color.

See this face?
        Wearing it like an accident
of birth.
    It was
a scar sealing up
a woman, now darkened
by desire.
        See this face?

Where do you take this hate
to lunch?

How
to get over
this one.

WINTER OF OPPRESSION, 1982

The cold in my chest comes
from having to decide

while the ice builds up on *this* side
of my new-york-apt.-bldg.-living window,
whose death
has been marked
upon the collective forehead
of this continent, this
shattering globe
the most indelibly.

Indelible. A catholic word
I learned
when I learned
that there were catholics and there
were not.
        But somehow
we did not count the Jews
among the have-nots, only protestants
with their cold & bloodless god
with no candles/no incense/no bloody
sacrifice or spirits
lurking.

Protestantism. The white people's
religion.

    ...

First time I remember
seeing pictures of the Holocaust
was in the tenth grade and the moving pictures
were already there in my mind
somehow *before* they showed me
what I already understood
that these people were killed

for the spirit-blood
that runs through them.

They were like us in this.
Ethnic people with long last names
with vowels at the end or the wrong
type of consonants
combined   a colored kind of white people.

But let me tell you
first time I saw an actual
picture glossy photo of a lynching
I was already grown & active
& living & loving Jewish.
Black. White. Puerto
Rican.
        And the image blasted
my consciousness
split it wide   I
had never thought   seen
heard   of such a thing
never even imagined the look
of the man   the weight
dead hanging swinging heavy
the fact   of the white people
cold bloodless
looking on   It

had never occurred to me
I tell you   I
the nuns failed to mention
this could happen, too
how *could* such a thing happen?

because somehow dark real dark
was not quite real
people killed
but some
thing not
taken to heart
in the same way it feels

to see white shaved/starved
burned/buried
the boned bodies stacked & bulldozed
into huge craters made by men
and machines
and at fifteen I counted 22
bodies only in the far left-hand
corner of the movie screen
& I kept running
through my mind
and I'm only one
count one
it could be me
it could be me
I'm nothing
to this cruelty.

    ...

Somehow tonight,
is it the particular coldness
where my lover sleeps with a scarf
to keep it out
that causes me to toss
and turn the events of the last weeks
the last years of my life
around in my sleep?

Is it the same white coldness
that forces my back up
against the wall—*choose.*
choose.

I cannot
choose nor forget

how simple
to fall back
upon rehearsed racial memory.

I work to remember
what I never dreamed possible

what my consciousness could never
contrive.

Whoever I am

I must believe
I am not
and will never be
the only
one
who suffers.

THE ROAD TO
RECOVERY

MINDS & HEARTS

the road to recovery
what was lost
in a war
that never pronounced itself

leaves no visible signs
no ration cards
sailor boys
ticker tape

parades, the road
to recovering what was lost
in a war that never pronounced
correctly

the road to recovering
what was lost in a war
that was never pronounced
dead
missing in
action, prisoner

of our minds
& hearts

NO BORN-AGAIN CHILDREN

"Somebody in my family just died!
Now are you gonna stay dead or pull a lazarus?"

Woman, if I could simply rise up
from this bed of doubt, miraculous and beaming,
I would.
       if I could,
       I would.

You told me that when your brother saw the train coming
he didn't move. He was   transfixed somehow
intensely curious   a boy of twelve with a body of pure
speed and a death wish
he's ready to dump   into the nearest river
or body that can swallow
it.
        He opened you up, pink and hungry, too
        but for the tenderness in his fingers talking
        you into, coaxing you into
        turning cold and quiet into you.

And taking the orange into your five-year-old fist
the boy coming at you again, you flung it out the window.

He stopped dead cold in his tracks.

I don't know why your brother died. I don't know why.
Was it the face of the orange, alive and bright, spinning
before his eyes? The vision of a girl
pushing life through the hole of doom that bore you both?

It *was* a suicide, woman. A suicide we both refuse
daily with all our good brains and tenderness. Still,

you can see me in him, can't you? Riveted onto that track
putting my cheek up against the size of a locomotive
just to see what it's like
just to taste how close it'll get before—

stone still & trembling
I split   off   that rail.

But I am not your brother. I will not die on you
no matter how you dare me
to reenact that tragedy
            like your momma dragging you down
            to the railroad tracks
            still hot from his suicide

            another child dead.

No, I will not die on you and yet, death keeps us
watching. We look to each other for miracles
to wipe out a memory full of dead men and dying
women, but we can't   save each other
from what we learned
to fear.

We can't

There are no miracles.
No Lazarus.
No born-again children.

Only an orange flung out of a window
like a life line that bears repeating
again and again
until we're both
convinced.

NOVEMBER AGAIN

she called it, *the black pearl* of my conviction
the security of knowing
at least our fear is unchangeable.

at the beach in november, there is a woman
with a thin silk robe draped around her bare shoulders
the rest of her bare, too, and a child coming after her.

naked on the beach and flaunting it, waving the silk
robe up around her head, leaping over its skirt, dancing.
the child humming to himself, like accompaniment.

three times, I imagine myself coming up to her,
taking her by the wrist, explaining to her
how she should cover up, not expose herself so,
not joyfully, like this.

passing the woman, I find a thin stone on the shore.
I lick the sand and salt clean from it, then rub it
dry and dull on the thigh of my pants.

leaving the beach, I place it in my pocket.

YOU CALL IT, *AMPUTATION*

(Macalister's boy took one of the fish and cut a square out of
its side to bait his hook with. The mutilated body (it was alive
still) was thrown back into the sea.)
—*To the Lighthouse*, Virginia Woolf

You call it
am pu tation

but even after the cut
they say the toes still itch
the body remembers the knee,
                                        gracefully bending

she reaches down to find her leg gone
the shape under the blanket dropping off
suddenly, irregularly

it is a shock, Woolf says
that by putting into words
we make it whole

still, I feel
the mutilated body
swimming in side stroke
pumping twice as hard
for the lack
of body, pushing
through your words
which hold no water
for me.

FOR AMBER

when her friend Yve died of a stroke

I want to catch it while it's still fresh
and living in you, this talking like
you don't know what's gonna come outta your mouth
next. I watch the bodies pour
right out between those red lips of yours
and without thinking, they're changing me
without trying, they're transforming
before my eyes.

I told you once
that you were like my grandmother
the white one, the gypsy
all dolled up
a white cadillac convertible
with Big Fins—she red deep
behind the wheel, her bleached blonde
flying. At stop lights she'd be there
just waiting for some sucker
to pull up, thinking she was
a gal of twenty. She'd turn
and flash him a seventy-year-old
smile, and press pedal.

Oh honey, this is you
in all your freeway glory,
the glamour of your ways.

And without stopping
last night you talked about the places
in you *thinking of your body*
that are lost to you, how we locate
that damage in our different parts

like a dead foot, you said, how we run
inventory—checking on which show
promise of revival
and which don't.

What I didn't tell you
was how my grandmother stopped
all of a sudden
turned baby, all of a sudden
speechless
my momma giving her baths
in the tub, while I played
her bare white skin slipping
down off those cold shoulders
piling up around her hips and knees,
slowing her down.

My grandma turned baby
and by the toilet I'd sit with her
she picking out designs in the linoleum
saying this one looks like a man
in a tub, scrubbing his back
with a brush,

and it did.

HEADING EAST

We are driving this car on determination, alone.

the miles seem to repair us
convince us that we are getting somewhere
that we won't have another breakdown

we end up leaking into somebody's movie
trapped in a ghost town   shaniko, oregon   pouring rain

we dive under the car
                    expose its underside, our fingers
feeling into the machine for its sore spot

"I've got it," I scream
"I know where the hole is." our eyes fire each other's

Thinking we have conquered the unknown
we patch up the lacerated hose with black tape.

                   ...

In this town of livery stable, turned museum
we roll out our bags onto the floor
of an abandoned caboose.

     we are *in* somebody's movie

Two women stranded in a ghost town.
They are headed east.
They think they'll make it.

MODERN DAY HERO

I would not have stopped, but there was the love that I wasn't getting from you which I had to put somewhere. Setting down the two six packs of beer onto the sidewalk, lifting up the head of the woman lying next to them.

A modern-day hero. If it takes heroism to win you back, then I guess that's what it takes.

Kay and I lift the woman into my car. "There, honey, you'll be fine." I hear her say for all of us, to each other. "There, honey, we got you....Yes, hold onto your purse."

That was how I found her, clutching her purse into her belly. Every other part of her limp, but her hands tight around her purse. And, there was a man with her—drunk like her—trying to get something out of her. Move her. Leave her. Take her purse. I don't know. All I know is that he's standing and she's face down with a mouth full of cement.

The police cars arrive. Some white man comes charging out of his house. "I called the police," he shouts, glad for himself. I could have throttled the guy, waving his hands over his head like a crazy person. *More men to contend with.*

The three of us, the woman, Kay and I, are getting quickly outnumbered. Two cars have pulled up with four cops inside. They pile out. There's only one brown one in the lot, but he's the one that says, looking at me, "Can you ladies get her home all right?" "Yes," I answer. And we do.

As the cop cars pull away and we pull the woman into my car, I can't get you clearly out of my mind. All along wondering how you could see me here, managing these men to save a woman. Lifting this woman up that long flight of stairs, home.

THE WARBRIDE

The minute we got back from Monterey Beach, sat down to table with two taquitos a piece laid out in front of us, I knew our relationship was on the road to recovery. The waitress, built like Tía Vicky—stocky, stick-legs, make-up & busy efficiency convinced me.

Who can survive the pacific ocean? When not bordered by 24th Street Mission-district storefronts. When not L.A. Venice Beach pre-redevelopment. When not simple like two sisters who knew the sun's setting into the water as the course of a day—no big deal, no romance, floating in a big black tube beyond the waves. Still counting on the fact that a mother would surely live forever—like a life forever wakening in the kitchen, cooking.

Who can survive the pacific ocean? Not in california. I know the beaches too well to fool you into thinking they are anything but fatal. It's not the water, exactly; it's what drives people to its edge. ROMANCE. SEX. MOMENTS OF QUIET CONTEM-PLATION. STEAK & LOBSTER & cliffside mansions owned by hollywood producers clinging to the canyon walls, praying *this* winter's mud will go around them.

"That rock is old," a friend said, "brittle and bitter. It was never meant to hold...," slipping away. But the beaches are about serious living, as if there were actually some huge neon splitting the orange atmosphere overhead as you barrel down highway one, warning: *Danger. Pacific Ocean Ahead. Check Your Life for Meaning.*

It's about taking stock. Makes sense now, in retrospect, how I would find my eyes so fixated on those stock piles of weapons the army used to store in big cement tombs on their beach front property just outside Monterey.

When I was a warbride, my boyfriend's job was to keep guard there, smoking joints. I wishing there was some *real* Vietnam he could object to, conscientiously. But I'd spread my legs for him anyway in seaside Motel 6's to relieve his misery that he was not out shooting shots & the shit with his dog and his buddies. And what else would I be doing anyway, if not spreading my thighs?

With you, it's supposed to be different and I guess it is when the beat of your hand against my bone/isn't worked against the beat of the water flooding memory/against the walls of my heart beating fast/against the flash of boys beating off, inside me.

LO QUE NUNCA PASÓ POR SUS LABIOS

A LONG LINE OF VENDIDAS

para Gloria Anzaldúa, in gratitude

Sueño: 15 de julio 1982

During the long difficult night that sent my lover and I to separate beds, I dreamed of church and cunt. I put it this way because that is how it came to me. The suffering and the thick musty mysticism of the catholic church fused with the sensation of entering the vagina—like that of a colored woman's—dark, rica, full-bodied. The heavy sensation of complexity. A journey I must unravel, work out for myself.

I long to enter you like a temple.

MY BROTHER'S SEX WAS WHITE. MINE, BROWN

If somebody would have asked me when I was a teenager what it means to be Chicana, I would probably have listed the grievances done me. When my sister and I were fifteen and fourteen, respectively, and my brother a few years older, we were still waiting on him. I write "were" as if now, nearly two decades later, it were over. But that would be a lie. To this day in my mother's home, my brother and father are waited on, including by me. I do this now out of respect for my mother and her wishes. In those early years, however, it was mainly in relation to my brother that I resented providing such service. For unlike my father, who sometimes worked as much as seventy hours a week to feed my face every day, the only thing that earned my brother my servitude was his maleness.

It was Saturday afternoon. My brother, then seventeen-years-old, came into the house with a pile of friends. I remember Fernie, the two Steves, and Roberto. They were hot, sweaty, and exhausted from an afternoon's basketball and plopped themselves down in the front room, my brother demanding, "Girls, bring us something to drink."

"Get it yourself, pig," I thought, but held those words from ever forming inside my mouth. My brother had the disgusting habit on these occasions of collapsing my sister, JoAnn's and my name when referring to us as a unit: his sisters. "Cher'ann," he would say. "We're really thirsty." I'm sure it took everything in his power *not* to snap his fingers. But my mother was out in the yard working and to refuse him would have brought her into the house with a scene before these boys' eyes which would have made it impossible for us to show our faces at school that following Monday. We had been through that before.

When my mother had been our age, over forty years earlier, she had waited on her brothers and their friends. And it was no mere lemonade. They'd come in from work or a day's drinking. And las mujeres, often just in from the fields themselves, would already be in the kitchen making tortillas, warming frijoles or pigs feet, albóndigas soup, what-have-you. And the men would get a clean white tablecloth and a spread of food laid out before their eyes and not a word of resentment from the women.

The men watched the women—my aunts and mother moving with the grace and speed of girls who were cooking before they could barely see over the top of the stove. Elvira, my mother, knew she was being watched by the men and loved it. Her slim hips moved patiently beneath the apron. Her deep thick-lidded eyes never caught theirs as she was swept back into the kitchen by my abuelita's call of "Elvirita," her brown hands deepening in color as they dropped back into the pan of flour.

I suppose my mother imagined that Joe's friends watched us like that, too. But we knew different. We were not blonde or particularly long-legged or "available" because we were "Joe's sisters." This meant no boy could "make" us, which meant no boy would bother asking us out. Roberto, the Guatemalan, was the only one among my brother's friends who seemed at all sensitive to how awkward JoAnn and I felt in our role. He would smile at us nervously, taking the lemonade, feeling embarassed being waited on by people he considered peers. He knew the anglo girls they visited would never have succumbed to such a task.

Roberto was the only recompense.

As I stopped to wait on their yearning throats, "jock itch" was all that came to my mind. Their cocks became animated in my head, for that was all that seemed to arbitrarily set us apart from each other and put me in the position of the servant and they, the served.

I wanted to machine-gun them all down, but swallowed that fantasy as I swallowed making the boy's bed every day, cleaning his room each week, shining his shoes and ironing his shirts before dates with girls, some of whom *I* had crushes on. I would lend him the money I had earned house-cleaning for twelve hours, so he could blow it on one night with a girl because he seldom had enough money because he seldom had a job because there was always some kind of ball practice to go to. As I pressed the bills into his hand, the car honking outside in the driveway, his double-date waiting, I knew I would never see that money again.

Years later, after I began to make political the fact of my being a Chicana, I remember my brother saying to me, "*I've* never felt 'culturally deprived'," which I guess is the term "white" people use to describe Third World people being denied access to *their* culture. At the time, I wasn't exactly sure what he meant, but I remember in re-telling the story to my sister, she responded, "Of course, he didn't. He grew up male in our house. He got the best of both worlds." And yes, I can see now that that's true. *Male in a man's world. Light-skinned in a white world. Why change?*

The pull to identify with the oppressor was never as great in me as it was in my brother. For unlike him, I could never have *become* the white man, only the white man's *woman*.

The first time I began to recognize clearly my alliances on the basis of race and sex was when my mother was in the hospital, extremely ill. I was eight years old. During my mother's stay in the hospital, my tía Eva took my sister and me into her care; my brother stayed with my abuela; and my father stayed by himself in our home. During this time, my father came to visit me and my sister only once. (I don't know if he ever visited my brother.) The strange thing was I didn't really miss his visits, although I sometimes fantasized some imaginary father, dark and benevolent, who might come and remind us that we still *were* a family.

I have always had a talent for seeing things I don't particularly want to see and the one day my father did come to visit us with his wife/our mother physically dying in a hospital some ten miles away, I saw that he couldn't love us—not in the way we so desperately needed. I saw that he didn't know how and he came into my tía's house like a large lumbering child—awkward and embarassed out of his league—trying to play a parent when he needed our mother back as much as we did just to keep him eating and protected. I hated and pitied him that day. I knew how he was letting us all down, visiting my mother daily, like a dead man, unable to say, "The children, honey, I held them. They love you. They think of you." Giving my mother *something.*

Years later, my mother spoke of his visits to the hospital. How from behind the bars of her bed and through the tubes in her nose, she watched this timid man come and go daily—going through the "motions" of being a husband. "I knew I had to live," she told us. "I knew he could never take care of you."

In contrast to the seeming lack of feeling I held for my father, my longings for my mother and fear of her dying were the most passionate feelings that had ever lived inside my young heart.

We are riding the elevator. My sister and I pressed up against one wall, holding hands. After months of separation, we are going to visit my mamá in the hospital. Mi tía me dice, "Whatever you do, no llores Cherrie. It's too hard on your mother when you cry." I nod, taking long deep breaths, trying to control my quivering lip.

As we travel up floor by floor, all I can think about is not crying, breathing, holding my breath. "¿Me prometes?" she asks. I nod again, afraid to speak fearing my voice will crack into tears. My sister's nervous hand around mine, sweating too. We are going to see my mamá, mamá, after so long. She didn't die after all. She didn't die.

The elevator doors open. We walk down the corridor, my heart pounding. My eyes are darting in and out of each room as we pass them, fearing/anticipating my mamá's face. Then as we turn around the corner into a kind of lobby, I hear my tía say to an older woman—skin and bones. An Indian, *I think, straight black and grey hair pulled back. I hear my tía say, "Elvira."*

I don't recognize her. This is not the woman I knew, so round and made-up with her hair always a wavy jet black! I stay back until she opens her arms to me—this strange and familiar woman—her voice hoarse, "¡Ay mi'jita!" Instinctively, I run into her arms, still holding back my insides—"Don't cry. Don't cry." I remember. "Whatever you do, no llores." But my tía had not warned me about the smell, the unmistakable smell of the woman, mi mama—el olor de aceite y jabón and comfort and home. "Mi mamá." And when I catch the smell I am lost in tears, deep long tears that come when you have held your breath for centuries.

There was something I knew at that eight-year-old moment that I vowed never to forget—the smell of a woman who is life and home to me at once. The woman in whose arms I am uplifted, sustained. Since then, it is as if I have spent the rest of my years driven by this scent toward la mujer.

> *when her india makes love*
> *it is with the greatest reverence*
> *to color, texture, smell*
>
> *by now she knew the scent of earth*
> *could call it up*
> *even between the cracks*
> *in sidewalks*
> *steaming dry*
> *from midday summer*
> *rain*

With this knowledge so deeply emblazed upon my heart, how then was I supposed to turn away from La Madre, La Chicana? If I were to build my womanhood on this self-evident truth, it is the love of the Chicana, the love of myself as a Chicana I had to embrace, no white man. Maybe this ultimately was the cutting difference between my brother and me. To be a woman fully necessitated my claiming the race of my mother. My brother's sex was white. Mine, brown.

LIKE A WHITE SHEEP I FOLLOWED

Sueño: 3 de julio

I am having my face made up, especially my eyes by a very beautiful Chicana. The make-up artist changes me entirely for only five dollars. I think this is a very low price for how deep and dark she makes me look.

When I was growing up, I looked forward to the days when I hoped my skin would toast to match my cousins, their skin turning pure black in the creases. I never could catch up, but my skin did turn smooth like theirs, oily brown—like my mamá's, holding depth, density, the possibility of infinite provision. Mi abuela raised the darkest cousins herself, she never wanting us the way she molded and managed them.

To write as a Chicana feminist lesbian, I am afraid of being mistaken, of being made an outsider again—having to fight the kids at school to get them to believe Teresita and I were cousins. "You don't *look* like cousins!" I feel at times I am trying to bulldoze my way back into a people who forced me to leave them in the first place, who taught me to take my whiteness and run with it. Run with it. Who want nothing to do with me, the likes of me, the white of me—in them.

When was I forced to choose? When Vivian Molina after two years of the deepest, richest friendship, two years of me helping her through "new math," helping her not flunk once more—once was enough—and her so big already, fat, and dark-skinned. When Vivian left me flat, I didn't know what happened, except I knew she was beginning to smell like a woman and once, just before our split-up, the neighbor-kid talked of Vivian growing hair "down there." I didn't get it, except I knew that none of these changes were settling right in Vivian. And I was small and thin, still, and light-skinned and I loved Vivian which didn't seem to matter in the way teachers were wondering if Vivian was going to make it through the year. So, one day that year Vivian came to school and never spoke to me again. Nothing happened between us. I swear nothing happened.

I would call her and plead, "Vivian, what did I do?" "Vivian, ¿por que?" I would have asked in Spanish if they had let me. "¿Qué pasó? No entiendo ¿Qué pasó?" But she never let on, except once when she nearly started to cry near the water fountain in the school corridor when I asked her for the last time and her eyes met mine finally and she said, I think or I'd like to remember, "I'm sorry." And even if she didn't say that, exactly, I know she said something that told me we were in different leagues now. And it couldn't be helped. It was out of our control. Something she, a year and a half older and much darker, knew before I knew and like a white sheep I followed the path paved for me.

Rocky Hernandez was brilliant and tough. Got mostly A's in school, like Carmen Luna who was her second cousin in the same grade. They were both wizards, but Rocky was sharper and mean in her sharpness. "Antagonistic," the nuns would say and she'd prove it in her handwriting which slanted way off to the left which I admired greatly, which the nuns found incorrigible. When it came time for the Catholic high school entrance exams, we learned in May what track we would be in for the coming freshman year. To my amazement, I got into the "A" group—college prep. To my equal amazement, Rocky and her cousin were tracked into the "C" group—business and general education where they teach you home economics and typing. Rocky could talk and write and compute circles around me, which didn't seem to compute on our entrance exams.

After we got into high school, the Irish and Italian girls became my friends. And Rocky and I seldom, if ever, spoke.

It was my mother, not my father, who fixed me on this idea of getting an education. "Without an education, you're nothing," she would say. "Look at me. If only I could write better, I could get a different kind of job, I wouldn't have to do the kind of work I do." She was constantly criticizing this or that younger aunt or uncle or in-law who had what she did not—basic reading and writing skills—who still worked factory. It never occurred to her, or if it did, she never let on to us children, that *color* was any factor in reducing one's chances for success.

And in terms of rearing her three light-skinned brown-haired children, we in fact did not have to fear, like my cousins, racial discrimination. On the surface of things we could pass as long as we made no point of our Chicano heritage. As long as we moved my father's name through our lives like a badge of membership to the white open-door policy club.

In fact, I had never fully realized until this year when I went back to California and the words tumbled out of my mouth to my sister, that color had anything to do with the reason my sister and brother and I were *the* success stories of the family. Within our sex, we have received the most education and work in recognized professions. I had acknowledged this inequity between myself and my mother's generation, but not within my own.

I remember my friend Tavo's words only two years ago, "You get to choose." He told me he didn't trust güeros, that we had to prove ourselves to him in some way. And you see I felt that challenge for proof laid out flat on the table between us.

So, I say, "Well, I understand that because it's awfully hard to be in this position under suspicion from so many." This constant self-scrutiny, digging deeper, digging deeper.

Then Tavo says to me, "You see at any time, if they (meaning me) decide to use their light skin privilege they can." I say, "Uh huh. Uh huh." He says, "You can decide you're suddenly no Chicano."

That I can't say, but once my light skin and good English saved me and my lover from arrest. And I'd use it again. I'd use it to the hilt over and over to save our skins.

"You get to choose." Now I want to shove those words right back into his face. You call this a choice! To constantly push up againt a wall of resistance from your own people or to fall away nameless into the mainstream of this country, running with our common blood?

But I *have* betrayed my people.

Rita Villareal and I used to go to the roller rink together. I never noticed how dark she was until my mother pointed this out to me, warning me against her. How her jet black straight hair and coffee bean skin marked her as a different grade of Mexicana. Una india, de clase baja. It was the first fight about race I ever had with my mother. When I protested, she said to me, "It isn't her color and I never tell you about your friends, but *this* girl is going to get you in trouble. She's no good for you." Our friendship soon broke off, me keeping a distance from Rita. Later, she got into boys and booze. *Was my mother right?*

Maybe this was what Vivian had feared/expected in me. My turning my back on her, like I had on Rocky.

Many years later when I was already in college, I had come home for the weekend and went on a short run to the supermarket for my mom. There, for the first time in at least three years, I ran into Rocky. She was pushing a shopping cart and inside it was one of the most beautiful baby boys I had ever laid eyes on, jabbering and wide-eyed.

Rocky and I talked. It was clear we both still felt some affection for each other from those early grade school days. I touched the kid's cheek, complimenting her on him. When she turned to enter the check-out line, I wanted to stop her, invite her to dinner, not let her out of my sight again. But I hesitated, wondering what we would have to say to each other after so many years. I let her go.

Driving home, I remembered that there had been rumors that Rocky was pregnant at graduation.

TRAITOR BEGETS TRAITOR

What looks like betrayal between women on the basis of race originates, I believe, in sexism/heterosexism. Chicanas begin to turn our backs on each other either to gain male approval or to avoid being sexually stigmatized by them under the name of puta, vendida, jota. This phenomenon is as old as the day is long, and first learned in the school yard, long before it is played out with a vengeance within political communities.

In the seventh grade, I fell in love with Manuel Poblano. A small-boned boy. Hair always perfectly combed and oiled. Uniform shirt pressed neatly over shoulder blades jutting out. At twelve, Manuel ws growing in his identity—sexually, racially— and Patsy Juárez, my one-time fifth-grade friend wanted him too. Manuel was pals with Leticia and Connie. I remember how they flaunted a school picture of his in front of my face, proving how *they* could get one from him, although I had asked first. The two girls were conspiring to get him to "go" with Patsy, which in the end, he finally did. I, knowing all along I didn't have a chance. Not brown enough. And the wrong last name.

At puberty, it seemed identity alliances were beginning to be made along rigid and immovable lines of race, as it combined with sex. And everyone—boy, girl, anglo, and Chicano—fell into place. Where did *I* stand?

I did not move away from other Chicanos because I did not love my people. I gradually became anglocized because I thought it was the only option available to me toward gaining autonomy as a person without being sexually stigmatized. I can't say that I was conscious of all this at the time, only that at each juncture in my development, I instinctively made choices which I thought would allow me greater freedom of movement in the future. This primarily meant resisting sex roles as much as I could safely manage and this was far easier in an anglo context than in a Chicano one. That is not to say that anglo culture does not stigmatize its women for "gender-transgressions"—only that its stigmatizing did not hold the personal power over me which Chicano culture did.

Chicanas' negative perceptions of ourselves as sexual persons and our consequential betrayal of each other finds its roots in a four-hundred year long Mexican history and mythology. It is further entrenched by a system of anglo imperialism which long ago put Mexicanos and Chicanos in a defensive posture against the dominant culture.

The sexual legacy passed down to the Mexicana/Chicana is the legacy of betrayal, pivoting around the historical/mythical female figure of Malintzin Tenepal. As translator and strategic advisor and mistress to the Spanish conqueror of México, Hernan Cortez, Malintzin is considered the mother of the mestizo people. But unlike La Virgen de Guadalupe, she is not revered as the Virgin Mother, but rather slandered as La Chingada, meaning the "fucked one," or La Vendida, sell-out to the white race.[1]

Upon her shoulders rests the full blame for the "bastardization" of the indigenous people of México. To put it in its most base terms: Malintzin, also called Malinche, fucked the white man who conquered the Indian peoples of México and destroyed their culture. Ever since, brown men have been accusing her of betraying her race, and over the centuries continue to blame her entire sex for this "transgression."

As a Chicana and a feminist, I must, like other Chicanas before me, examine the effects this myth has on my/our racial/sexual identity and my relationship with other Chicanas. There is hardly a Chicana growing up today who does not suffer under her name even if she never hears directly of the one-time Aztec princess.

The Aztecs had recorded that Quetzalcoatl, the feathered serpent god, would return from the east to redeem his people in the year One Reed according to the Aztec calendar. Destiny would have it that on this very day, April 21, 1519 (as translated to the Western calendar), Cortez and his men, fitting the description of Quetzalcoatl, light-haired and bearded, landed in Vera Cruz.[2]

At the time of Cortez's arrival in México, the Aztecs had subjugated much of the rest of the Indian population, including the Mayans and Tabascans, who were much less powerful militarily. War was a necessity for the Aztecs in order to take prisoners to be used for sacrificial offerings to the warrior-god, Huitzilopochtli. As slaves and potential sacrificial victims to the Aztecs, then, these other Indian nations, after their own negotiations and sometimes bloody exchanges with the Spanish, were eager to join forces with the Spanish to overthrow the Aztec empire. The Aztecs, through their systematic subjugation of much of the Mexican Indian population, decreed their own self-destruction.[3]

Aleida Del Castillo, Chicana feminist theorist, contends that as a woman of deep spiritual commitment, Malinche aided Cortez because she understood him to be Quetzalcoatl returned in a different form to save the peoples of México from total extinction. She writes, "The destruction of the Aztec empire, the conquest of México, and as such, the termination of her indigenous world," was, in Malinche's eyes, "inevitable" in order to make way for the new spiritual age that was imminent.[4]

Del Castillo and other Chicana feminists who are researching and re-interpreting Malinche's role in the conquest of México are not trying to justify the imperialism of the Spanish. Rather, they are attempting to create a more realistic context for, and therefore a more sympathetic view of, Malinche's actions.

The root of the fear of betrayal by a woman is not at all specific to the Mexican or Chicano. The resemblance between Malinche and the Eve image is all too obvious. In chronicling the conquest of México and founding the Catholic Church there, the Spanish passed on to the mestizo people as legacy their own European-Catholic interpretation of Mexican events. Much of this early interpretation originated from Bernal del Castillo's eye-witness account of the conquest. As the primary source of much contemporary analysis as well, the picture we have of Mexican Indian civilization during that period often contains a strong Catholic and Spanish bias.

In his writings, Bernal Diaz del Castillo notes that upon the death of Malinche's father, the young Aztec princess was in line to inherit his estate. Malinche's mother wanted her son from her second marriage to inherit the wealth instead. She therefore sold her own daughter into slavery.

According to Gloria Anzaldúa, there are writings in México to refute this account.[5] But it was nevertheless recorded—or commonly believed—that Malinche was betrayed by her own mother. It is this myth of the inherent unreliability of women, our natural propensity for treachery, which has been carved into the very bone of Mexican/Chicano collective psychology.

Traitor begets traitor.

Little is made of this early betrayal, whether or not it actually occurred, probably because no man was immediately affected. In a way, Malinche's mother would only have been doing her Mexican wifely duty: *putting the male first.*

There is none so beautiful as the Latino male. I have never met any kind of Latino who, although he may have claimed his family was very woman-dominated ("mi mamá made all the real decisions"), who did not subscribe to the basic belief that men are better. It is so ordinary a statement as to sound simplistic and I am nearly embarrassed to write it, but that's the truth in its kernel.

Ask, for example, any Chicana mother about her children and she is quick to tell you she loves them all the same, but she doesn't. *The boys are different.* Sometimes I sense that she feels this way because she wants to believe that through her mothering, she can develop the kind of man she would have liked to have married, or even have been. That through her son she can get a small taste of male privilege, since without race or class privilege that's all there is to be had. The daughter can never offer the mother such hope, straddled by the same forces that confine the mother. As a result, the daughter must constantly earn the mother's love, prove her fidelity to her. The son—he gets her love for free.

After ten years of feminist consciousness and activism, why does this seem so significant to me—to write of the Mexican mother favoring the son? I think because I had never quite gone back to the source. Never said in my own tongue, *the boys, they are men, they can do what they want...after all, he's a man.*

Journal Entry: April 1980

Three days ago, my mother called me long distance full of tears, loving me, wanting me back in her life after such a long period of separation. My mother's tears succeed in getting me to break down the edge in my voice. the protective distance. My mother's pleading "mi'jita, I love you, I hate to feel so far away from you." succeed in opening my heart again to her.

I don't remember exactly why my heart had been shut, only that it had been very necessary to keep my distance, that in a way we had agreed to that. But, it only took her crying to pry my heart open again.

I feel myself unriveting. The feelings begin to flood my chest. Yes, this is why I love women. This woman is my mother. There is no love as strong as this, refusing my separation, never settling for a secret that would split us off, always at the last minute, like now, pushing me to brink of revelation, speaking the truth.

I am as big as a mountain! I want to say, "Watch out, Mamá! I love you and I am as big as a mountain!" And it is on the brink of this precipice where I feel my body descending into the places where we have not spoken, the times I did not fight back. I am descending, ready to speak the truth, finally.

And then suddenly, over the phone, I hear another ring. My mother tells me to wait. There is a call on my father's work phone.

Moments later, "It is your brother," she says. My knees lock under me, bracing myself for the fall...Her voice lightens up. "Okay, mi'jita. I love you. I'll talk to you later," cutting off the line in the middle of the connection.

I am relieved when I hang up that I did not have the chance to say more. The graceful reminder. This man doesn't have to earn her love. My brother has always come first.

Seduction and betrayal. Since I've grown up, no woman cares for me for free. There is always a price. My love.

What I wanted from my mother was impossible. It would have meant her going against Mexican/Chicano tradition in a very fundamental way. You are a traitor to your race if you do not put the man first. The potential accusation of "traitor" or "vendida" is what hangs above the heads and beats in the hearts of most Chicanas seeking to develop our own autonomous sense of ourselves, particularly through sexuality. Even if a Chicana knew no Mexican history, the concept of betraying one's race through sex and sexual politics is as common as corn. As cultural myths reflect the economics, mores, and social structures of a society, every Chicana suffers from their effects. And we project the fear onto each other. We suspect betrayal in one another— first to other men, but ultimately and more insidiously, to the white man.

Journal Entry: noviembre 1980
...this white man coming up over and over again. There's something about him that feels like such a suck to me. And so I ask myself, is it only that my Chicana mother fed my white father all the days of her life? Is it this model I am struck with/stuck with? The white man getting the attention that should go to the Chicana daughters, that should be shared between women?

I don't sense within our culture the same fear of a man betraying our race. It is the woman who is the object of our contempt. We can't ultimately hold onto her, not in the cosmic sense. She who could provide us with the greatest sense of belonging is never truly ours; for she is always potential chattel for the white man. As with so many of our mothers, my mother's relationship with white men made survival for her and her family possible.

It was Mr. Bowman who saved the day. Saved the day in Tijuana. Big white businessman Mr. Bowman. Not very good-looking, but did he need to be? Had money. A very good dresser, mi mamá would say. The second wife, a mexicana—or was that his mistress? No recuerdo, pero this was a man to be counted on.

Cuando se murió mi abuelo, he gave mamá the bucks for the funeral. Mi abuela never asking where it came from. Mi mamá said to me, "She didn't care how I got it. How did she think I got it. I was only a girl, hija, a girl."

'Bout the time she got to the Foreign Club, they were both older. He was no spring chicken, never, even in the early years, but by now she was close to eighteen and he thought, after all, it's about time.

The chauffeur, a Mexicano, put them into the back seat of the big blue sedan and they all began their way down the coast toward Rosarita Beach. Mi mamá prayin the entire way, prayin "santo niño madre de dios san antonio"...you name it, she brought out every saint and holy person she could think of, but focusing, of course, on her patron, San Antonio. Running the rosary beads through her mind, she prayed, "san antonio, por favor, ayúdeme."

She had seen the chauffeur fill the tank with gas. They had all gone to the station together. She remembered that. She had seen him fill it up. But there they were, her prayin between snatches of conversation, Big Bowman sitting next to her, pleased with himself, and the car starts sputtering and jerking to a stop. They were out of gas. Smack in the desert.

It was a day's journey back to town.

No gas. No hotel. No Rosarita. No sex with Mr. Bowman.

That time the saints saved her.

"He never laid a hand on me. It wasn't that he didn't want to," she said, "but I was very lucky. If he would of wanted me, what could I do? But I was very lucky."

So little has been documented as to the actual suffering Chicanas have experienced resisting or sucumbing to the sexual demands of white men. The ways we have internalized the sexual hatred and exploitation they have displayed against us are probably too numerous and too ingrained to even identify. If the Chicana, like her brother, suspects other women of betrayal, then she must, in the most profound sense, suspect herself. How deep her suspicions run will measure how ardently she defends her commitment, above all, to the Chicano male. As obedient sister/daughter/lover she is the committed heterosexual, the socially acceptable Chicana. Even if she's politically radical, sex remains the bottom line on which she proves her commitment to her race.

WE FIGHT BACK WITH OUR FAMILIES

Because heterosexism*—the Chicana's sexual commitment to the Chicano male—is proof of her fidelity to her people, the Chicana feminist attempting to critique the sexism in the Chicano community is certainly between a personal rock and a political hard place.

Although not called "the sexism debate," as it has been in the literary sectors of the Black movement, the Chicano discussion of sexism within our community has like that movement been largely limited by heterosexual assumption: "How can we get our men right." The feminist-oriented material which appeared in the late 70s and early 80s for the most part strains in its attempt to stay safely within the boundaries of Chicano—male-defined and often anti-feminist—values.

Over and over again, Chicanas trivialize the women's movement as being merely a white middle-class thing, having little to offer women of color. They cite only the most superficial

*The term "heterosexism" deserves a definition here as it, like "homophobia," has seldom, if ever, appeared in Chicano publications. Heterosexism is the view that heterosexuality is the "norm" for all social/sexual relationships and as such the heterosexist imposes this model on all individuals through homophobia (fear of homosexuality). S/he supports and/or advocates the continued institutionalization of heterosexuality in all aspects of society—including legal and social discrimination against homosexuals and the denial of homosexual rights as a political concern.

aspects of the movement. For example, in "From Woman to Woman," Silvia S. Lizarraga writes:

> ...class distinction is a major determinant of attitudes toward other subordinated groups. In the U.S. we see this phenomenon operating in the goals expressed in the Women's Liberation Movement.... The needs represent a large span of interests—from those of *capitalist women*, women in business and professional careers, to *witches* and *lesbians*. However, the needs of the unemployed and working class women of different ethnic minorities are generally overlooked by this movement.[6] (my emphasis)

This statement typifies the kind of one-sided perspective many Chicanas have given of the women's movement in the name of Chicana liberation. My question is *who* are they trying to serve? Certainly not the Chicana who is deprived of some very critical information about a ten-year grassroots feminist movement where women of color, including lesbians of color (certainly in the minority and most assuredly encountering "feminist" racism) have been actively involved in reproductive rights, especially sterilization abuse, battered women's shelters, rape crisis centers, welfare advocacy, Third World women's conferences, cultural events, health and self-help clinics and more.

Interestingly, it is perfectly acceptable among Chicano males to use white theoreticians, e.g. Marx and Engels, to develop a theory of Chicano oppression. It is unacceptable, however, for the Chicana to use white sources by women to develop a theory of Chicana oppression. Even if one subscribes to a solely economic theory of oppression, how can she ignore that over half of the world's workers are female who suffer discrimination not only in the workplace, but also at home and in all the areas of sex-related abuse I just cited? How can she afford not to recognize that the wars against imperialism occurring both domestically and internationally are always accompanied by the rape of women of color by both white and Third World men? Without a feminist analysis what name do we put to these facts? Are these not deterrents to the Chicana developing a sense of "species being?" Are these "women's issues" not also "people's issues?" It is far easier for the Chicana to criticize white women who on the face of things could never be familia, than to take issue with or complain, as it were, to a brother, uncle, father.

The most valuable aspect of Chicana theory thus far has been its re-evaluation of our history from a woman's perspective through unearthing the stories of Mexican/Chicana female figures that early on exhibited a feminist sensibility. The weakness of these works is that much of it is undermined by what I call the "alongside-our-man-knee-jerk-phenomenon." In speaking of María Hernández, Alfredo Mirande and Evangelina Enríquez offer a typical disclaimer in *La Chicana*:

> Although a feminist and leader in her own right, she is always quick to point to the importance of family unity in the movement and to acknowledge the help of her husband..."[7]

And yet we would think nothing of the Chicano activist never mentioning the many "behind-the-scenes" Chicanas who helped him!

In the same text, the authors fall into the too-common trap of coddling the Chicano male ego (which should be, in and of itself, an insult to Chicano men) in the name of cultural loyalty. Like the Black Super-woman, the Chicana is forced to take on extra-human proportions. She must keep the cultural home-fires burning while going out and making a living. She must fight racism alongside her man, but challenge sexism single-handedly, all the while retaining her "femininity" so as not to offend or threaten *her man*. This is what being a Chicana feminist means.

In recent years, however, truly feminist Chicanas are beginning to make the pages of Chicano, feminist, and literary publications. This, of course is only a reflection of a fast-growing Chicana/Third World feminist movement. I am in debt to the research and writings of Norma Alarcón, Martha Cotera, Gloria Anzaldúa, and Aleida Del Castillo, to name a few.* Their work reflects a relentless commitment to putting the female first, even when it means criticizing el hombre.[8]

*In acknowledging these few women, I think of so many other Chicanas and other Latina feminists who were the very first in their political activism to bring up the issue of our particular oppression as brown

To be critical of one's culture is not to betray that culture. We tend to be very righteous in our criticism and indictment of the dominant culture and we so often suffer from the delusion that, since Chicanos are so maligned from the outside, there is little room to criticize those aspects from within our oppressed culture which oppress us.

I am not particularly interested in whether or not Third World people learned sexism from the white man. There have been great cases made to prove how happy men and women were together before the white man made tracks in indigenous soil. This reflects the same mentality of white feminists who claim that all races were in harmony when the "Great Mother" ruled us all. In both cases, history tends to prove different. In either case, the strategy for the elimination of racism and sexism cannot occur through the exclusion of one problem or the other. As the Combahee River Collective, a Black feminist organization, states, women of color experience these oppressions simultaneously."[9] The only people who can afford not to recognize this are those who do not suffer this multiple oppression.

I remain amazed at how often so-called "Tercermundistas" in the U.S. work to annihilate the concept and existence of white supremacy, but turn their faces away from male supremacy. Perhaps this is because when you start to talk about sexism, the world becomes increasingly complex. The power no longer breaks down into neat little hierarchical categories, but becomes a series of starts and detours. Since the categories are not easy to arrive at, the enemy is not easy to name. It is all so difficult to unravel. It *is* true that some men hate women even in their desire for them. And some men oppress the very women they love. But unlike the racist, they allow the object of their contempt to share the table with them. The hatred they feel for women does not translate into separatism. It is more insidiously intra-cultural, like class antagonism. But different, because it lives and breathes in the flesh and blood of our families, even in the name of love.

women. Speaking up in isolation, ten and fifteen years ago, without a movement to support them, these women had little opportunity to record their own history of struggle. And yet, it is they who make this writing and the writing of my compañeras possible.

In Toni Cade Bambara's novel, *The Salt Eaters,* the curandera asks the question, *Can you afford to be whole?*"[10] This line represents the question that has burned within me for years and years through my growing politicization. *What would a movement bent on the freedom of women of color look like?* In other words, what are the implications of not only looking outside of our culture, but into our culture and ourselves and from that place beginning to develop a strategy for a movement that could challenge the bedrock of oppressive systems of belief globally?

The one aspect of our identity which has been uniformly ignored by every existing political movement in this country is sexuality, both as a source of oppression and a means of liberation. Although other movements have dealt with this issue, sexual oppression and desire have never been considered specifically in relation to the lives of women of color. Sexuality, race, and sex have usually been presented in contradication to each other, rather than as part and parcel of a complex web of personal and political identity and oppression.

Female sexuality must be controlled, whether it be through the Church or the State. The institutions of marriage and family, and necessarily, heterosexuality, prevail and thrive under capitalism as well as socialism. Patriarchal systems of whatever ilk must be able to determine how and when women reproduce. For even "after the revolution," babies must be made, and until they find a way of making them without us (which is not that far off into the future), we're here for the duration. In China, for example, married couples are now being mandated by the State to limit their children to one. Abortions are not only available, but women are sometimes forced by family and friends to undergo an abortion or meet with severe economic recriminations from the State. In the U.S., the New Right's response to a weakening economic system, which they attribute in part to women's changing position in the family, is to institute legislation to ensure governmental control of women's reproductive rights. Unlike in China, however, the New Right is "morally" opposed to abortion. The form their misogyny takes is the dissolution of government-assisted abortions for the poor, bills to limit teenage girls' right to birth control, and the advocacy of the Human Rights Amendment, which allows the fetus greater right to life than the mother. These backward political moves hurt all women, but most especially the poor and "colored."

The white man's so-called "benevolent protection" of the family and the role of women within it has never extended to the woman of color. She is most often the victim of enforced pregnancy and sterilization. She is always the last to "choose."

Unlike most white people, with the exception of the Jews, Third World people have suffered the threat of genocide to our races since the coming of the first European expansionists. The family, then, becomes all the more ardently protected by oppressed peoples, and the sanctity of this institution is infused like blood into the veins of the Chicano. At all costs, la familia must be preserved: for when they kill our boys in their own imperialist wars to gain greater profits for American corporations; when they keep us in ghettos, reservations, and barrios which ensure that our own people will be the recipients of our frustrated acts of violence; when they sterilize our women without our consent because we are unable to read the document we sign; when they prevent our families from getting decent housing, adequate child care, sufficient fuel, regular medical care; then we have reason to believe—although they may no longer technically be lynching us in Texas or our sisters and brothers in Georgia, Alabama, Mississippi—they intend to see us dead.

So we fight back, we think, with our families—with our women pregnant, and our men, the indisputable heads. We believe the more severely we protect the sex roles within the family, the stronger we will be as a unit in opposition to the anglo threat. And yet, our refusal to examine *all* the roots of the lovelessness in our families is our weakest link and softest spot.

Our resistance as a people to looking at the relationships within our families—between husband and wife, lovers, sister and brother, father, son, and daughter, etc.—leads me to believe that the Chicano male does not hold fast to the family unit merely to safeguard it from the death-dealings of the anglo. Living under Capitalist Patriarchy, what is true for "the man" in terms of misogyny is, to a great extent, true for the Chicano. He, too, like any other man, wants to be able to determine how, when, and with whom his women—mother, wife, and daughter—

110

are sexual. For without male imposed social and legal control of our reproductive function, reinforced by the Catholic Church, and the social institutionalization of our roles as sexual and domestic servants to men, Chicanas might very freely "choose" to do otherwise, including being sexually independent *from* and/or *with* men. In fact, the forced "choice" of the gender of our sexual/love partner seems to precede the forced "choice" of the form (marriage and family) that partnership might take. The control of women begins through the institution of hetero-sexuality.

Homosexuality does not, in and of itself, pose a great threat to society. Male homosexuality has always been a "tolerated" aspect of Mexican/Chicano society, as long as it remains "fringe." A case can even be made that male homosexuality stems from our indigenous Aztec roots.[11] But lesbianism, in any form, and male homosexuality which openly avows both the sexual and emotional elements of the bond, challenges the very foundation of la familia.*

The question remains. Is the foundation as it stands now sturdy enough to meet the face of the oppressor? I think not. There is a deeper love between and amongst our people that lies buried between the lines of the roles we play with each other. It is the earth beneath the floor boards of our homes. We must split wood, dig bare-fisted into the packed ground to find out what we really have to hold in our hands as muscle.

Family is *not* by definition the man in a dominant position over women and children. Familia is cross-generational bonding, deep emotional ties between opposite sexes, and within our sex. It is sexuality, which involves, but is not limited to, intercourse or orgasm. It springs forth from touch, constant and daily. The ritual of kissing and the sign of the cross with every coming and going from the home. It is finding familia among friends where blood ties are formed through suffering and celebration shared.

The strength of our families never came from domination. It has only endured in spite of it—like our women.

* The "faggot" is the object of the Chicano/Mexicano's contempt because he is consciously choosing a role his culture tells him to despise. That of a woman.

111

LA MALINCHISTA

Chicanos' refusal to look at our weaknesses as a people and a movement is, in the most profound sense, an act of self-betrayal. The Chicana lesbian bears the brunt of this betrayal, for it is she, the most visible manifestation of a woman taking control of her own sexual identity and destiny, who so severely challenges the anti-feminist Chicano/a. What other reason is there than that for the virtual dead silence among Chicanos about lesbianism? When the subject *is* raised, the word is used pejoratively.

For example, Sonia A. López writes about the anti-feminism in El Movimiento of the late 60s:

> The Chicanas who voiced their discontent with the organizations and with male leadership were often labeled "women's libbers," and "lesbians." This served to isolate and discredit them, a method practiced both covertly and overtly."[12]

This statement appears without qualification. López makes no value judgment on the inherent homophobia in such a divisive tactic. Without comment, her statement reinforces the idea that lesbianism is not only a white thing, but an insult to be avoided at all costs.

Such attempts by Chicana feminists to bend over backwards to prove criticism of their people is love (which, in fact, it is) severely undermines the potential radicalism of the ideology they are trying to create. Not quite believing in their love, suspecting their own anger, and fearing ostracism from Chicano males (being symbolically "kicked out of bed" with the bait of "lesbian" hanging over their work), the Chicana's imagination often stops before it has a chance to consider some of the most difficult, and therefore, some of the most important, questions.

It is no wonder that the Chicanas I know who *are* asking "taboo" questions are often forced into outsiderhood long before they begin to question el carnal in print. Maybe like me they now feel they have little to lose.

It is important to say that fearing recriminations from my father never functioned for me as an obstacle in my political work. Had I been born of a Chicano father, I sometimes think I

112

never would have been able to write a line or participate in a demonstration, having to repress all questioning in order that the ultimate question of my sexuality would never emerge. Possibly, even some of my compañeras whose fathers died or left in their early years would never have had the courage to speak out as Third World lesbians the way they do now, had their fathers been a living part of their daily lives. The Chicana lesbians I know whose fathers are very much a part of their lives are seldom "out" to their families.

During the late 60s and early 70s, I was not an active part of la causa. I never managed to get myself to walk in the marches in East Los Angeles (I merely watched from the sidelines); I never went to one meeting of MECHA on campus. No soy tonta. I would have been murdered in El Movimiento—light-skinned, unable to speak Spanish well enough to hang; miserably attracted to women and fighting it; and constantly questioning all authority, incuding men's. I felt I did not belong there. Maybe I had really come to believe that "Chicanos" were "different," not "like us," as my mother would say. But I fully knew that there was a part of me that was a part of that movement, but it seemed that part would have to go unexpressed until the time I could be a Chicano and the woman I had to be, too.

The woman who defies her role as subservient to her husband, father, brother, or son by taking control of her own sexual destiny is purported to be a "traitor to her race" by contributing to the "genocide" of her people—whether or not she has children. In short, even if the defiant woman is *not* a lesbian, she is purported to be one; for, like the lesbian in the Chicano imagination, she is una *Malinchista*. Like the Malinche of Mexican history, she is corrupted by foreign influences which threaten to destroy her people. Norma Alarcón elaborates on this theme of sex as a determinant of loyalty when she states:

> The myth of Malinche contains the following sexual possibilities: woman is sexually passive, and hence at all times open to potential use by men whether it be seduction or rape. The possible use is double-edged: that is,the use of her as pawn may be intracultural—"amongst us guys" or intercultural, which means if we are not using her then

"they" must be using her. Since woman is highly pawnable, nothing she does is perceived as choice.[13]

Lesbianism can be construed by the race then as the Chicana being used by the white man, even if the man never lays a hand on her. *The choice is never seen as her own.* Homosexuality is *his* disease with which he sinisterly infects Third World people, men and women alike. (Because Malinche is female, Chicano gay men rebelling against their prescribed sex roles, although still considered diseased, do not suffer the same stigma of traitor.) Further, the Chicana lesbian who has relationships with white women may feel especially susceptible to such accusations, since the white lesbian is seen as the white man's agent. The fact that the white woman may be challenging the authority of her white father, and thereby could be looked upon as a potential ally, has no bearing on a case closed before it was ever opened.

The first dyke I remember in school was Sally Frankel, whom everyone called "Frank," the way she liked it. She could play the meanest game of four-square of them all—built lean and solid as an eighth grade boy, and smart too. And very, very clearly white. *Were all lesbians white?* I remember thinking that I had never quite met a girl like Frank before—so bold, somehow freer than the rest of us. She was an "army brat" and so had lived many places, even in Europe. While all my Chicana friends were leaving me high and dry for the guys, this girl—although not particularly interested in me—represented a life beyond the tight group discussions of girls, locked arm-in-arm, where the word "chinga" was dropped like a slug in my throat. (Even at fourteen, I was still to wonder if I could get pregnant slow-dancing with a boy, picking up my knowledge of sex from these cryptic conversations.) The desire I felt for women had nothing and everything to do with the vulgarity of intercourse; had nothing and everything to do with the dreams that wracked my bed at night. Somehow Frank connected with all this—as did the "funny couple" I had encountered surreptitiously one hot afternoon a few years before.

At the time we were living in the Kenwood Hotel, a kind of "drifter" hang-out, down on Main Street in Huntington Beach, long before there was any development there. Just a few bars, a little drugstore, "The Paddock" restaurant, and a surfboard shop. My mom was managing the place.

One day I was making my way down the long hallway to go play out on the big sundeck when I suddenly stopped short of the screen door. Some "new" people were out there who were not the "regulars." Hiding behind the screen door, I decided to observe.

One woman looked like a Marilyn Monroe type—50s style. Her hair was brassy blonde and in a kind of permanent wave. Her yellow sundress was very tight around her waist and low-cut. The other person next to her I knew was really a woman, although she looked mostly like a man: white dress shirt with sleeves rolled up, pack of cigs in her front breast pocket, black men's trousers. She was a pretty big woman, about twice the size of Marilyn, except her head was small—dark haired and greased back.

Marilyn had her dress hiked up above her knees and between her thighs she had put an open jar of Skippy peanut butter. I watched the two women as she dipped the knife into the jar, pulled out a thick glob of the brown mass, then ran her tongue along it luxuriously like she had all day to eat the stuff. She then gave it to the other one to lick in the same place. All I could think about were the germs that were being passed back and forth.

The next day, I learned that the "funny" women in room six had sneaked out in the middle of the night without paying. They had stolen the alarm clock too. My momma said she had tried to give them the benefit of the doubt, but "never again." *Were all lesbians white? And decent ladies, Mexican? Who was I in this?*

But it was the Mexican women I had loved first.

Sandra García and I used to make out after school. I think we mostly put a pillow between our faces so our lips wouldn't touch, but our bodies would get all enwrapped with each other. At eleven, Sandra was already "stacked" and, very innocently, we would take the role of movie stars—she playing Deborah Walley and me, James Darren, lusting after each other. Sandra's young body seemed a miracle of womanhood to me, the bow of her pink brassiere always cropping up out between the opening of her too-small white uniform blouse.

I wanted Sandra and as long as she was interested, I'd throw myself up on the couch with her and make out until my cheeks were sore.

My cousin Teresa and I made out too; and this was for real. Making up stories about shipwrecks and sailor/saviors of young French women, we would shut ourselves up in our abuelita's bedroom and press our lips long and hard against each other. One time we touched tongues which I remember so delighted us that we even demonstrated this to my mom who happened into the bedroom. "Mira, tía," Teresita said, and we touched tongues tip-to-tip and giggled uproariously. My mother, of course, reprimanded us immediately and it was only then that I realized that the strange sensation running through me had something to do with "down there." Our games soon came to an end, my feeling guilty for taking advantage of my cousin three years younger than me.

But I can see now that these experiences with Sandra and Teresa were brief moments of sexual connection with other Chicanas that were to be systematically denied me for the next twenty years of my life.

The Mexican women in my life, a pain I don't want to get to.

It seems my life has always been a kind of Catch 22. For any way you look at it, Chicana's are denied one another's fidelity. If women betray one another through heterosexism, then lesbianism is a kind of visible statement of our faithfullness to one another. But if lesbianism is white, then the women I am faithful to can never be my own. And we are forced to move away from our people. As Gloria Anzaldúa once said to me, "If I stayed in Hargill, I would never have been able to be myself. I had to leave to come out as the person I really was." And if I had stayed in the San Gabriel Valley, I would have been found for dead, at least the walking dead.

I have always known too much. It was too clear to me—too tangible—too alive in the breath of my nose, the pulse in my thighs, the deep exhales that flowed from my chest when I moved into a woman's arms.

116

Journal Entry: primavera 1980

I don't know what happened to make me this way. I do fear for my life sometimes. Not that a bullet would hit my brain, but that I will forget to be afraid of the enemy. I dreamed last night of a hostility in me so great that on the job I put a pen through the skull of a white man. I have felt like an outcast on my job lately. The new manager wants to fire me for my "politics." I am a lesbian. I love women to the point of killing for us all.

An old friend came to visit me yesterday. She is leaving her good husband for the wild love of a woman. We were both very sad together. Not for the separation from her husband but for so many years of separation from women.

Some people try to convince me that the secrets I hold about loving women do not put me in a position of threat to my life. You see, you can't see this condition—this posture of mind and heart and body—in the movement of my joints or on the surface of my skin. And then again, sometimes you can. But I know they are wrong.

I feel very threatened and very threatening...

My mother does not worry about me; she fears me. She fears the power of the life she helped to breathe into me. She fears the lessons she taught me will move into action. She fears I might be willing to die rather than settle for less than the best of loving.

The line of reasoning goes:

Malinche sold out her indio people by acting as courtesan and translator for Cortez, whose offspring symbolically represent the birth of the bastardized mestizo/Mexicano people. My mother then is the modern-day Chicana, Malinche marrying a white man, my father, to produce the bastards my sister, my brother, and I are. Finally, I—a half-breed Chicana—further betray my race by *choosing* my sexuality which excludes all men, and therefore most dangerously, Chicano men.

I come from a long line of Vendidas.

I am a Chicana lesbian. My own particular relationship to being a sexual person; and a radical stand in direct contradiction to, and in violation of, the women I was raised to be.

117

INOCENCIA MEANT DYING RATHER THAN BEING FUCKED

Coming from such a complex and contradictory history of sexual exploitation by white men and from within our own race, it is nearly earth-shaking to begin to try and separate the myths told about us from the truths; and to examine to what extent we have internalized what, in fact, is not true.

Although intellectually I knew different, early-on I learned that women were the willing cooperators in rape. So over and over again in pictures, books, movies, I experienced rape and pseudo-rape as titillating, sexy, as what sex was all about. Women want it. Real rape was dark, greasy-looking bad men jumping out of alleys and attacking innocent blonde women. Everything short of that was just sex; the way it is: dirty and duty. We spread our legs and bear the brunt of penetration, but we do spread our legs. In my mind, inocencia meant dying rather than being fucked.

I learned these notions about sexuality not only from the society at large, but more specifically and potently from Chicano/ Mexicano culture, originating from the myth of La Chingada, Malinche. In the very act of intercourse with Cortez, Malinche is seen as having been violated. She is not, however, an innocent victim, but the guilty party—ultimately responsible for her own sexual victimization. Slavery and slander is the price she must pay for the pleasure our culture imagined she enjoyed. In *The Labyrinth of Solitude*, Octavio Paz gives an explanation of the term "chingar," which provides valuable insights into how Malinche, as symbolized by La Chingada, is perceived. He writes:

> The idea of breaking, of ripping open. When alluding to a sexual act, violation or deception gives it a particular shading. The man who commits it never does so with the consent of the chingada...
>
> Chingar then is to do violence to another, i.e., rape. The verb is masculine, active, cruel: it stings, wounds, gashes, stains. And it provokes a bitter, resentful satisfaction. The person who suffers this action is passive, inert, and open, in contrast to the active, aggressive, and closed person who

inflicts it. The chingón is the macho, the male; he rips open the chingada, the female, who is pure passivity, defenseless against the exterior world.[14]

If the simple act of sex then—the penetration itself—implies the female's filthiness, non-humaness, it is no wonder Chicanas often divorce ourselves from the conscious recognition of our own sexuality. Even if we enjoy having sex, draw pleasure from feeling fingers, tongue, penis inside us, there is a part of us that must disappear in the act, separate ourselves from realizing what it is we are actually doing. Sit, as it were, on the corner bedpost, watching the degradation and violence some "other" woman is willing to subject herself to, not us. And if we have lesbian feelings—want not only to be penetrated, but to penetrate—what perverse kind of monstrosities we must indeed be! It is through our spirits that we escape the painful recognition of our "base" sexual selves.

When I was about twelve years old, I had the following dream:

I am in a hospital bed. I look down upon my newly-developing body. The breasts are large and ample. And below my stomach, I see my own cock, wildly shooting menstrual blood totally out of control. The image of the hermaphrodite.

In another context, I could have seen this dream as a very sexually potent vision, reflecting a desire for integration, wholeness. But in my child's imagination, I am incapable of handling such information emerging from my unconscious. Up to that point I always knew that I felt the greatest emotional ties with women, but suddenly I was beginning to consciously identify those feelings as sexual. The more potent my dreams and fantasies became and the more I sensed my own exploding sexual power, the more I retreated from my body's messages and into the region of religion.

By giving definition and meaning to my desires, religion became the discipline to control my sexuality. Sexual fantasy and rebellion became "impure thoughts" and "sinful acts."

I was raised within a very strict brand of Mexican, mixed with anglo, Catholicism. This was in many ways typical for

Chicano children whose parents are of my mother's generation. We were taught by the Irish nuns to seek the love and forgiveness of the Father. But after confession, I went straight home to my mother, knelt before her and asked pardon for my sins against her. It seemed the real test was to kneel down on the flesh and bones of your knees, to be relieved by lágrimas, by un besito en la cocina de mi mamá.

I remember once in the seventh grade, we were having a religion class on "doubting the existence of God." I had been doubting for years, as the fact of the matter was, that there was a god to be touched. Whoever He was, was becoming increasingly remote as the touch of men began to fall hungrily upon my body, awkwardly like they didn't know what they wanted. The touch of women was like fire in my veins. God had never actually once forgiven me, but my mother had.

I confess that it was during this class as the nun proceeded to describe the various forms of atheism...it was at this point for some unspeakable reason that I saw my life for a moment like a flash of revelation that filled me with horror. I pictured myself lying flat on my back on a kind of surgery table and people—like white doctors—stood around my body, putting dreams in my head. The dream that made up my life—the people, the sensations, the emotions that gripped my heart. All these things were no more than figures in my imagination, thoughts that formed pictures of bodies that could not actually be touched. Love in this case was impossible. I was crucially and critically alone and powerless.

In retrospect, I see this fantasy as a revelation, on one hand, and on the other, the beginning of the way I was to learn to cope with my burgeoning sexuality. The revelation was that, yes, in fact, the Chicana *is* manipulated by a white God-Father, white president-father, under whose jurisdiction she is nearly powerless and alienated from the dominant society. In a way, the fantasy was a foreshadowing of what oppression awaited me as a young Chicana growing into womanhood.

The coping mechanism is more difficult to describe, but I see now that in order not to embody the *chingada,* nor the femalized, and therefore perverse, version of the *chingón*, I became pure spirit—bodiless. For what, indeed, must my body look like if I were both the *chingada* and the *chingón?*

In my early adolescence, my fears moved me further and further away from the living, breathing woman-in-the-flesh and closer and closer to the bodiless god. The confessions of box and curtain cloth. The strange comfort that the church would be standing there, just around the turn from the cemetery. That it would be expecting me—grand, square, predictable as stone. That the end of mass would find a palm placed in my hand. The sure knowledge of the spines of leaf bending into my grip.

The comfort and terror of powerlessness.

La niña chooses this time not to kneel in the pew. Having started for her knees, she breaks the bend, scooting back against the hard-boned wood of the pew bench: "O-my-gaw-i'm-hartly-sorry..." No. the child chooses this time not to begin this way. Breaking the line, she says nothing. Waiting, she lets the visions come.

Y los diablos begin to parade before her. As common to her now as the space she'd grown to picture like flesh between her rib cage—the place where she thought her soul to sleep. Thinking white, thinking empty, thinking quiet, clean and untouched. It was this spot she protected from the advancing intruders: blood-pumping, wild-eyed things. The parts of men, like animals rearing, ramming into anything that could swallow them. The parts of women, quartered, stripped, and shamed.

La niña shook the pictures from her mind, intervening before they could slip below and infect the sacred place inside her chest. She, the caretaker of her soul. The warrior. The watchdog, overburdened, beaten by now.

No resistance. Not this time. Not lifting her eyes, she only looked into her hands, repeating to herself, "just look at your hands," repeating as the only language she would allow herself until words slipped from her altogether, until she knew only the touch of her red, cold hands against the thighs of her uniform skirt, until she knew only her body, without fire, her face dropped between her knees, her arms wrapped 'round her thin calves rocking, rocking, rocking...

Forgive us, Father, for how badly we need tenderness.

How does one describe a world where the mind twists like a rag dry of any feeling? Only an absent inarticulate terror. A mouth hung open with no voice breaking through?

When I was nineteen, I lost my virginity. It was during those early years of heterosexual activity that the estranged feelings of outsiderhood revisited me. In awakening to the touch of a man, my sexual longings for women, which I had managed to suppress since puberty, re-surfaced. The sheer prospect of being a lesbian was too great to bear, fully believing that giving into such desires would find me shot-up with bullets or drugs in a gutter somewhere. Further, although I physically found sex with men very satisfying, I couldn't quite look at what I was doing, having turned against my church and my mother in the act. Instead I began to develop fantasies about it. Like the white doctor visions of my childhood, I became in my imagination a dark and sinister priestess. Her flowing robes of toads and sequins draped loosely over my naked shoulders. Her menacing laugh fell hungrily from my lips whenever I saddled up upon my boyfriend's lap, riding him. The first time I felt the feeling coming out from behind my heart and through my open legs, gripping the bone of the boy wanting me, I fell into deep sobbing. I remembered I had felt this somewhere, sometime before. I had waited nearly ten years holding my breath back between my pursed lips, now remembering...

...when as a child without touching myself, the pain that tugged gently at my ovaries (not maliciously, but only with an alive sense of their existence), the pressure I felt in my bowels, and the heat in my lower back—all comingled into a delicious kind of pleasure.

Today it has a name. At eleven, I only hoped for the return of the strange uncontrollable feeling. It was an *accident* of pleasure. I wondered if other girls got this feeling too. If my sister, one year older, ever did. If it was a fact of growing up, like the thick red dirt smudge of blood that I had only months before found on my underpants.

I barely touched myself, except in the beginning when the feeling first occurred, my fingers instinctively moving down to the place where the slightest amount of pressure drew the sensation deep from out of the pit of my stomach and into my vagina in cool streams of relief. If I held my knees together tight enough to feel the lips puffed and throbbing between them, the feeling would sometimes replay itself in echoes of kindly, calling voices—momma voices—growing more and more faint as they departed.

"Mi'jita...Chorizito...Hijita..."

Months later, or was it years, my mother warned after I had spent some time locked in the bathroom that it was not good to push yourself too hard when you were trying to "go." She mentioned "piles," but not knowing what that was, I figured she knew about the pleasure, the pain, the pushing brought on and it was bad. It was years later before I ever reenacted my private bathroom ritual again.

Only occasionally, through high school, pretending it wasn't quite happening, I would sit with one foot under me, placing the wedge of the sole of my hard oxford school shoes up between my labia. For hours, I would allow myself at least this secret comfort through t.v. shows and homework late into the night, my sister on the other side of the dining room table.

At what point does the fear become greater than the flesh and the flesh of the fantasy prevail?

The more vividly the sinister priestess fantasies appeared to me, the more viciously I would fuck to obliterate them from my mind. I was always wanting sex: in cars, behind the bleachers of the neighborhood ball park, my boyfriend and I breaking into the park office where he worked to use its floor. Somehow I felt that if I fucked long and hard enough, I might being to *feel* again.

Occasionally, I would go through days, sometimes a week, of reprieve from these obsessions, but they would never last. Seemingly without my control, I could be in a conversation with someone and begin to feel as though I were being sucked down into a hole in the ground where I could always still *see* the person, shrinking, but they grew further and further away from my hearing. Their body framed by the lip of the tunnel I had fallen into. Their mouth moving soundlessly. These feelings of outsiderhood became the lens through which I saw most of my waking life, like a thin film between me and the people I longed to touch, to reach to for help.

we never spoke again, really
after the time I pulled up in front
of our mother's house, hands still
on the wheel
    Sister, I need
to talk with you and told her
there was a devil on my tail
riding me.

I know she saw it clear as me
I know she'd seen it in my younger years
always creeping too close to her, like I was
some crazy infection,

and I guess I am, crazy
that catches.

In my "craziness" I wrote poems describing myself as a centaur: half-animal/half-human, hairy-rumped and cloven-hoofed, como el diablo. The symbols emerged from a deeply Mexican and Catholic place.

My recurring sense of myself outside the normal life and touch of human beings was again, in part, a kind of revelation. A foreshadowing of the marginal place, within my culture and in society at large, my sexuality was to eventually take me.

Sometimes a breakdown can be the beginning of a kind of break-through, a way of living in advance through a trauma which prepares you for a future of radical transformation. The third time I broke was many years after I had stopped seeing men. I had been out as a lesbian for a while and had examined, I thought, what this made me in the world at large, but I had never actually looked into the eyes of what this made me in the world of my cultural community. Since I was so busy making room simply to live a lesbian life safely—coming out to my family, friends, at school, in print, to my employers, etc., I had never wrestled with the reality of what being a *Chicana* lesbian meant.

All this changed, however, when I thought I saw in a lover, a woman, the chingón that I had so feared to recognize in myself: "the active, aggressive and closed person," as Paz writes, "who inflicts [the wound]." I had met my match. I was forced to confront how, in all my sexual relationships I had resisted, at all costs, feeling la chingada which, in effect, meant that I had resisted fully feeling sex at all. *Nobody wants to be made to feel the turtle with its underside all exposed, just pink and folded flesh.* In the effort to avoid embodying la chingada, I became the chingón. In the effort not to feel fucked, I became the fucker, even with women. In the effort not to feel pain or desire, I grew a callous around my heart and imagined I felt nothing at all.

What I never quite understood until this writing is that to be without a sex—to be bodiless—as I sought to be to escape the burgeoning sexuality of my adolescence, my confused early days of active heterosexuality, and later my panicked lesbianism, means also to be without a race. I never attributed my removal from physicality to have anything to do with race, only sex, only desire for women. And yet, as I grew up sexually, it was my race, along with my sex, that was being denied me at every turn.

I was plagued with sexual contradictions. Lesbianism as a sexual act can never be construed as reproductive sex. It is not work. It is purely about pleasure and intimacy. How this refutes, spits in the face of, the notion of sex as rape, sex as duty! In stepping outside the confines of the institution of heterosexuality, I was indeed *choosing* sex freely. *The lesbian as institutionalized outcast.*

During those years as an active feminist lesbian, I became increasingly aware of the fact that *my* sexuality had not only made me an outcast from my culture, but if I seriously listened to it, with all its specific cultural nuances, it would further make me an outcast from the women's movement—a movement which I had run to for dear life to avoid the gutter I had feared was waiting for me. With no visible Third World feminist movement in sight, it seemed to me to be a Chicana lesbian put me far beyond the hope of salvation.

TIRED OF THESE ACTS OF TRANSLATION

What the white women's movement tried to convince me of is that lesbian sexuality was *naturally* different than heterosexual sexuality. That the desire to penetrate and be penetrated, to fill and be filled, would vanish. That retaining such desires was "reactionary," not "politically correct," "male-identified." And somehow reaching sexual ecstasy with a woman lover would never involve any kind of power struggle. Women were different. We could simply magically "transcend" these "old notions," just by seeking spiritual transcendence in bed.

The fact of the matter was that all these power struggles of "having" and "being had" were being played out in my own bedroom. And in my psyche, they held a particular Mexican twist. White women's feminism did little to answer my questions. As a Chicana feminist my concerns were different. As I wrote in 1982:

> What I need to explore will not be found in the feminist lesbian bedroom, but more likely in the mostly heterosexual bedrooms of South Texas, L.A., or even Sonora, México. Further, I have come to realize that the boundaries white feminists confine themselves to in describing sexuality are based in white-rooted interpretations of dominance, submission, power-exchange, etc. Although they are certainly *part* of the psychosexual lives of women of color, these boundaries would have to be expanded and translated to fit my people, in particular, the women in my family. And I am tired, always, of these acts of translation.[15]

Mirtha Quintanales corroborates this position and exposes the necessity for a Third World feminist dialogue on sexuality when she states:

> The critical issue for me regarding the politics of sexuality is that as a Latina Lesbian living in the U.S., I do not really have much of an opportunity to examine what constitutes sexual conformity and sexual defiance in my own culture, in my own ethnic community, and how that may affect my own values, attitudes, sexual life *and* politics. There is virtually no dialogue on the subject anywhere and I, like other Latinas and Third World women, especially Lesbians, am quite in the dark about what we're up against besides negative feminist sexual politics.[16]

During the late 70s, the concept of "women's culture"

among white lesbians and "cultural feminists" was in full swing; it is still very popular today. "Womon's history," "wommin's music," "womyn's spirituality," "wymyn's language," abounded—all with the "white" modifier implied and unstated. In truth, there was/is a huge amount of denial going on in the name of female separatism. Women do not usually grow up in women-only environments. Culture is sexually-mixed. As Bernice Reagon puts it:

> ...we have been organized to have our primary cultural signals come from factors other than that we are women. We are not from our base, acculturated to be women people, capable of crossing our first people boundaries: Black, White, Indian, etc.[17]

Unlike Reagon, I believe that there are certain ways we *have* been acculturated to be "women people," and there is therefore such a thing as "women's culture." This occurs, however, as Reagon points out, within a context formed by race, class, geography, religion, ethnicity, and language.

I don't mean to imply that women need to have men around to feel at home in our culture, but that the way one understands culture is influenced by men. The fact that some aspects of that culture are indeed oppressive does not imply, as a solution, throwing out the entire business of racial/ethnic culture. To do so would mean risking the loss of some very essential aspects of identity, especially for Third World women.

Journal Entry: julio 1981
New England. Boston to be exact. Pouring summer rain. We are all immigrants to this town—una hermana de Chicago, una de Tejas, una de Puerto Rico, y yo, de California. And the four of us move out into the rain under the beat of the downpour on the roof of the porch. Cooling off from the evening of enchiladas. I make up a little concoction of a summer drink: jugo de naranja, tequila, limón. Tossing in all kinds of ice cubes, "Try this," I say.

Y mis hermanas drink it up. Dos chicanas y dos puerto-riqueñas getting a little high from the food and the rain and the talk, hablando de nuestras madres.

Sitting out on the porch that night, what made me at home and

filled me with ease where I forgot about myself in a fine and fluid
way was not just that the Spanish sounds wrapped around the
English like tortillas steaming in flour sacks, not just that we all
had worked hard to get here from hard-working homes, not just that
we understood the meaning of familia, but that we were women—
somos mujeres. This is what women's culture means to me.

In failing to approach feminism from any kind of materialist
base, failing to take race, ethnicity, class into account in deter-
mining where women are at sexually, many feminists have
created an analysis of sexual oppression (often confused with
sexuality itself) which is a political dead-end. "Radical Femi-
nism," the ideology which sees men's oppression of women as
the root of and paradigm for all other oppressions allows women
to view ourselves as a class and to claim our sexual identity as
the *source* of our oppression and men's sexual identity as the
source of the world's evil. But this ideology can never then fully
integrate the concept of the "simultaneity of oppression" as
Third World feminism is attempting to do. For, if race and class
suffer the woman of color as much as her sexual identity, then
the Radical Feminist must extend her own "identity" politics to
include her "identity" as oppressor as well. (To say nothing of
having to acknowledge the fact that there are men who may
suffer more than she.) This is something that for the most part,
Radical Feminism as a movement has refused to do.

Radical Feminist theorists have failed to acknowledge how
their position in the dominant culture—white, middle-class,
often Christian—has influenced every approach they have taken
to implement feminist political change—to "give women back
their bodies." It follows then that the anti-pornography move-
ment is the largest organized branch of Radical Feminism. For
unlike battered women's, anti-rape, and reproductive rights
workers, the anti-porn "activist" never has to deal with any live
woman outside of her own race and class. The tactics of the
anti-pornography movement are largely symbolic and theoreti-
cal in nature. And, on paper, the needs of the woman of color are a
lot easier to represent than in the flesh. Therefore, her single-
issued approach to feminsm remains intact.

It is not that pornography is not a concern to many women of color. But the anti-materialist approach of this movement makes little sense in the lives of poor and Third World women. Plainly put, it is our sisters working in the sex industry.

Many women ivolved in the anti-porn movement are lesbian separatists. Because the Radical Feminist critique is there to justify it, lesbianism can be viewed as the logical personal response to a misogynist political system. Through this perspective, lesbianism has become an "idea"—a political response to male sexual aggression, rather than a sexual response to a woman's desire for another women. In this way, many ostensibly heterosexual women who are not active sexually can call themselves lesbians. Lesbians "from the neck up." This faction of the movement has grown into a kind of cult. They have taken whiteness, class privilege, and an anglo-american brand of "return-to-the-mother" which leaps back over a millenium of patriarchal domination, attempted to throw out the man, and call what is left female. While still retaining their own racial and class-biased cultural superiority.

The lesbian separatist retreats from the specific cultural contexts that have shaped her and attempts to build a cultural-political movement based on an imagined oppression-free past. It is understandable that many feminists opt for this kind of asexual separatist/spiritualist solution rather than boldly grappling with the challenge of wresting sexual autonomy from such a sexually exploitative system. Every oppressed group needs to imagine through the help of history and mythology a world where our oppression did not seem the pre-ordained order. Aztlán for Chicanos is another example. The mistake lies in believing in this ideal past or imagined future so thoroughly and single-mindedly that finding solutions to present-day inequities loses priority, or we attempt to create too-easy solutions for the pain we feel today.

As culture—our race, class, ethnicity, etc.—influences our sexuality, so too does heterosexism, marriage, and men as the primary agents of those institutions. We can work to tumble those institutions so that when the rubble is finally cleared away we can see what we have left to build on sexually. But we can't ask a woman to forget everything she understands about sex in a heterosexual and culturally-specific context or tell her what she is allowed to think about it. Should she forget and not use what she knows sexually to untie the knot of her own desire, she may lose any chance of ever discovering her own sexual potential.

FEEDING PEOPLE IN ALL THEIR HUNGERS

History has taught us that the effectiveness of a movement often depends on its ability to provide what, at least, feels at the time like a spiritual imperative. Spirituality which inspires activism and, similarly, politics which move the spirit—which draw from the deep-seated place of our greatest longings for freedom—give meaning to our lives. Such a vision can hold and heal us in the worst of times, and is in direct opposition to an apolitical spiritualist view of the world or a totally materialistic perspective.

The Civil Rights Movement is probably the best recent example in this country of a movement that was able to to reach masses of people through its spiritually-uplifting vision. The power of that vision, however, was based on the fact that in a very profound sense, it was deeply rooted in Black culture, and therefore, of necessity, Black spirituality. Religious fervor was not manufactured for the purposes of social or revolutionary change, but instead grew directly out of Black people's experience, influencing all those who became a part of that movement.

Major missing elements in the Civil Right Movement, however, were consciousness and activism around specifically female and sexual concerns, as well as an understanding of the entrenchedness of white power and how to move against it. Although the race-related movements that jumped off from the Civil Rights Movement in the late 60s, such as the American Indian Movement, La Raza, and Black Power were thoroughly coming to terms with the extent and depth of white power, the role of women of color was neither subject for debate nor activism except as women functioned as female members of the race.

But times have changed. The women's movement and lesbian and gay liberation movements in the 70s brought both the subject of women's rights and sexuality, respectively, to the political light of day. Furthermore, in the 80s with the increasing conservatism of the country manifested in the reign of Reagan and the rise of the Moral Majority, Third World organizations and organizers can no longer safely espouse the family and, therefore, homophobia, as the righteous *causa* without linking themselves with the most reactionary, and by definition, the most racist political sectors of this county.

The emergence of Third World feminism, then, seemed imminent. Third World lesbians' disillusionment with the racism and classism of the women's and gay movements and the sexism and homophobia of Third World movements did much to force us to begin to organize ourselves autonomously in the name of Third World feminism.

If any movement, however, could provide a "spiritual" reference point for Third World feminism, it would be the Civil Rights Movement in its culturally-based, anti-separatist, and "humanist" (not to be confused with liberal) approach to political change. As Barbara Smith, Black feminist activist and writer, explains:

> I was trying to figure out what the connection was/is for me between the Civil Rights movement and the Black Feminist movement. It is among other things, this. That the Civil Rights movement was based upon the concept of love and deep spirituality. It was a movement with a transcendent vision. *A movement whose very goal was to change the impossible, what people thought could not be changed.*
>
> The women's movement has some of these same qualities, a belief in the human. Actually Black Feminism is a kind of divine coalescing of the two because as Black women we have an identity and therfore a politics that requires faith in the humaness of Blackness and femaleness. We are flying in the face of white male conceptions of what humaness is and proving that it is not them, but us.
>
> That's what the Civil Rights movement was getting to through its divine patience and fortitude—although tactically and strategically it was, at times, flawed—the constant demonstration that we are really the human ones.

131

Black feminism, lesbian feminism in particular, moves in that direction...We will show you what it means to be human, what it means to really care about humanity.[18]

As a Chicana who grew up in a very religious household, I learned early on to respect the terrain of the spirit as the place where some of the most essential aspects of one's life are enacted. The spirit world—my sleeping dreams, my waking fantasies, my prayers and compulsive preoccupations—was and is very rich for me. A place from which I derive strength and perseverance. A place where much internal torture has taken place.

Women of color have always know, although we have not always wanted to look at it, that our sexuality is not merely a physical response or drive, but holds a crucial relationship to our entire spiritual capacity. Patriarchal religions—whether brought to us by the colonizer's cross and gun or emerging from our own people—have always known this. Why else would the female body be so associated with sin and disobedience? Simply put, if the spirit and sex have been linked in our oppression, then they must also be linked in the strategy toward our liberation.

To date, no liberation movement has been willing to take on the task. To walk a freedom road that is both material and metaphysical. Sexual and spiritual. Third World feminism is about feeding people in all their hungers.

BRINGING THE STRAINS TOGETHER*

Contrary to popular belief among Chicanos, Chicana Feminism did not borrow from white feminists to create a movement. If any direct "borrowing" was done, it was from Black feminists.

In 1977, the Combahee River Collective wrote: "The most profound and potentially most radical politics come directly out of our own identity." They go on to say that they "are committed to struggling against racial, sexual, heterosexual, and class oppression and see as [their] particular task, the development of

* Parts of this section originally appeared in a speech I gave at the Second National Third World Lesbian and Gay Conference in Chicago in November 1981. It was entitled, "A Unified Rainbow of Strength."

integrated analysis and practice based upon the fact that the major systems of oppression are interlocking."[19]

This "Black Feminist Statement" had considerable impact in creating an analysis of U.S. Third World women's oppression. It first appeared in *Capitalist Patriarchy: A Case for Socialist Feminism*, edited by Zillah Eisenstein, and has been reprinted numerous times in leaflet form and in other feminist publications. When I first discovered it in 1978, there were three things that struck me the most profoundly: one was the lesbian visibility of its authors; second was their expressed solidarity with other women of color; and third was a concern for what might be considered the *psycho-sexual* oppression of women of color. The statement asserts: "We are all damaged people merely by virtue of being Black women."[20]

The appearance of these sisters' words *in print*, as lesbians of color, suddenly made it viable for me to put myself in the center of a movement. I no longer had to postpone or deny any part of my identity to make revolution easier for somebody else to swallow.

I had heard too many times that my concern about specifically sexual issues was divisive to the "larger struggle" or wasn't really the "primary contradiction" and therefore, not essential for revolution. That to be concerned about the sexuality of women of color was an insult to women in the Third World literally starving to death. But the only hunger I have ever known was the hunger for sex and the hunger for freedom and somehow, in my mind and heart, they were related and certainly not mutually exclusive. If I could not use the source of my hunger as the source of my activism, how then was I to be politically effective? But finally here was a movement, first voiced by U.S. Black women, which promised to deal with the oppression that occurred *under* the skin as well, and by virtue of the fact that that skin was female and colored. For the damage that has been done to us sexually has penetrated our minds as well as our bodies. The existence of rape, the veil, genital mutilation, violence against lesbians, have bludgeoned our entire perception of ourselves as female beings.

As Barbara Smith writes, "It is Third World feminism that is bringing the strains together."[21]

One of the major components of Black feminism is that women of color embody the coalition essential for revolution and that each form of oppression, including that which occurs outside of material conditions, is part and parcel of a larger political scheme. What women of color suffer in our families and relationships is, in some way, inherently connected to the rape of women in our neighborhoods, the high suicide rate of American Indians on reservations, attacks on Black gays and disabled people in New York City bars, and the war in El Salvador. Whether one death is sexually motivated and the other the result of U.S. imperialism, women of color are always the potential victims.

Each movement then that tries to combat an aspect of women of color's oppression offers an organized strategy for change that women of color cannot afford to ignore. The difference now is that as we begin to organize and create our own programs and institutions, we are building a political base so that we will no longer have to fall prey to the tokenism and invisibility we have encountered in other movement work. Without the political autonomy of oppressed groups, coalition politics are a bankrupt notion.

But organizing ourselves is no easy task. The homophobia of heterosexual sisters and the racism among us cross-culturally are two major obstacles toward our being a unified movement. To begin with, we are profoundly ignorant about one another's cultures, traditions, languages, particular histories of oppression and resistance, and the cultural adaptations each people has had to make in the face of total cultural obliteration. But even this would only be a matter of education, if our prejudices against one another had only penetrated our minds, and not also our hearts.

Quite simply, the oppression of women of color, especially as we have internalized it, holds the greatest threat to our organizing successfully together, intra-culturally as well as cross-culturally. I think what is hardest for any oppressed people to understand is that *the sources of oppression form not only our radicalism, but also our pain.* Therefore, they are often the places we feel we must protect unexamined at all costs.

Recently, I was strutting down the street in my neighborhood in Brooklyn when I caught, out of the side view of my eye, the sight of an old Irish woman with a garbage bag about the same size as her. She was trying to maneuver this huge thing down the ten steps which made up the stoop to her building. "Want some help?" I stop. And she gladly accepts, touching my cheek in thank you, telling God to bless me at least three times until I finally settle the bag there by its fellows at the bottom of the stoop. I move on down the street, feeling like the good child I was raised up to be. Then the thought came and turned the pleasantness of the encounter—the "isn't-it-good-to-be-alive-and-in-new-york" feeling—cold in my chest. I thought, *if you looked as colored as you think, she'd maybe not let you close enough to help her. The first gesture of the open hand, seen by the woman as a move to attack/you see the fear in her face/your hand closes up/your heart. You soon learn not to volunteer your help.*

Oppression. Let's be clear about this. Oppression does not make for hearts as big as all outdoors. Oppression makes us big and small. Expressive and silenced. Deep and Dead.

Even the economic restraints seem to be less of a deterrent to our successful organizing than this more insidious, invisible obstacle. The more desperate the economic times, the greater our incentive is to challenge the system simply to put bread on the table. In do-or-die situations, women of color can be relied upon to throw ourselves down in the face of fire for family. Our instincts are solidly in the right place. But on a daily basis, have we learned to take the race hatred, the class antagonism, the fear of our fiery sexual passion and not beat ourselves down with it, not maintain our place with it, not keep one another in line with it?

Journal Entry: June 1981

And we line the women we love along the tips of our fingers, counting five to ten of the most dangerous brave women we know and we want to crawl under a rock, each.

You see, to take a stand outside of face-to-face crisis, outside of dying for your children, outside of "Bolt me, Dueño, outta my house? Well, Cabrón, I'll show you." And she takes a sledge hammer from the neighbor's yard and blows her way back into her home.

We'll eat beans, but we'll eat! And nobody's throwing us out!"

This stand we understand. The power is plain.

But after our bellies are full, our children well-fed and grown. After we've learned to walk with our face exposed having beaten off the man who tried to beat it one too many times. After we've learned to stand alone. Known loneliness and born it as a matter of course. Been nearly convinced not to expect a damn thing better from your people or yourself. Learned these lessons ten and twenty times over and still come up kicking, then what?

"Our survival is our contribution to our struggle," a South African woman freedom fighter once said.

But what of passion? I hunger to ask. There's got to be something more than hand-to-mouth survival.

MORE THAN HAND TO MOUTH SURVIVAL

The right to passion expressed in our own cultural tongue and movements is what this essay seems, finally, to be about. I would not be trying to develop some kind of Chicana feminist theory if I did not have strong convictions, urgent hunches, and deep racial memory that the Chicana could *not* betray a sister, a daughter, a compañera in the service of the man and his institutions if somewhere in the chain of historical events and generations, she were allowed to love herself as both female and mestiza.

What might our relationships with one another look like if we did not feel we had to protect ourselves from the violent recriminations of our fathers, brothers, bosses, governors? What might our sexuality look like? Audre Lorde, Black lesbian poet, writes:

> ...In order to perpetuate itself, every oppression must corrupt or distort those various sources of power within the culture of the oppressed that can provide energy for change.[22]

The extent to which our sexuality and identity as Chicanas have been distorted both within our culture and by the dominant culture is the measure of how great a source of our potential power it holds. We have not been allowed to express ourselves in specifically female and Latina ways or even to explore what those ways are. As long as that is held in check, so much of the rest of our potential power is as well.

I cannot stomach the twists sexual repression takes in the Latina. It makes us too-hot-to-handle. Like walking fire hazards, burning bodies in our paths with the singe of our tongues, or the cut of our eyes. Sex turned manipulation, control—which ravages the psyche, rather than satisfy the yearning body and heart.

In the wee hours of the morning my lover and I fight. We fight and cry and move against each other and a torrent of pain. The pain doesn't stop. We do not shout at midnight. We have learned to keep our voices down. In public. In the public ear of the building where we try to build a home. We fight quietly, urgently. The latina who lives below us—who catches sight of us in the hall and turns her pale cheek away from us, whose eyes are the eyes of my enemy—is pounding on the ceiling. Again. A frantic hateful beating below us, under our bed. She knows we are up, up to something. She hates us. And my lover's eyes staring back at me are red like apples from tears. The pounding—more vicious—continues. Our neighbor wants to remind us. She is there with her husband, her children in the next room. Decent people sleep at this hour. My lover says, "We are two women. We have no right to care so much about each other that the pain could keep us up."

"Those women—or whatever they are," she describes us to the lady next door the next morning.

If they hurt me, they will hurt me in that place. *The place where I open my mouth to kiss and something primordial draws the lips back, cause a woman to defend herself against the love of a woman.*

I am everybody's pesadilla. Jota. Pata. Dyke. Walking through the rooms of my friends' house, her grown son says to her, "Don't you let her (meaning me) put her hands on you." He fears his mami's eye will turn on him. To me. To me. For once, mujer, turn to me. Choose. Choose me. Cara a cara con el hombre.

The distortion and repression of our sexuality is so commonplace a fact in our lives that as young Chicanas we learn to accept it as "culturally natural" as we grow into womanhood. In a letter on my thirtieth birthday, my sister wrote to me:

> I remember the shock when you slowly began to need a bra. I can see you wearing that T-shirt I brought you from Arizona—two little round mounds sticking out from under the shirt. And mom mentioned that after she had rubbed you down, she had been surprised to find two tiny hairs sprouting. I hated to hear her speak of it. As a painfully growing adolescent, I hoped that you, who always looked like such a child, would be spared the curses I was having to face.

Is it possible to build a movement that grapples with *this* kind of suffering? The "damage" the Third World woman suffers, as the Combahee River Collective describes it? The visibility of Third World feminist lesbians choosing our sexual partner against the prescribed cultural norms and our examining the political implications of such a choice can provide, I believe, the kind of political space necessary for other women of color to begin to ask themselves some profound and overdue questions about their own psycho-sexual identity. The Third World lesbian brings colored female sexuality with all its raggedy edges and oozing wounds—for better or for worse—into the light of day.

I once had a very painful conversation with my mother—a conversation about moving away from her. I am the only person—male or female—among my relatives who ever left home for good without getting married first. My mother told me that she felt in some way that I was choosing my "friends" (she meant lesbian lovers) over her. She said, "No one is ever going to love you as much as I do. No one." We were both crying by then and I responded, "I know that. I know. I know how strong your love is. Why do you think I am a lesbian?"

Dead silence. But I knew, I felt in the air, that it was the silence of an unspeakable recognition. Of understanding finally, what my being a lesbian meant to me. I had been "out" to my mother for years, but not like this.

I knew at that moment that this kind of thing has happened for generations among Chicanas. It is our tradition to conceive of the bond between mother and daughter as paramount and essential in our lives. It is the daughters that can be relied upon. Las hijas who remain faithful a la madre, a la madre de la madre.

When we name this bond between the women of our race, from this Chicana feminism emerges. For too many years, we have acted as if we held a secret pact with one another never to acknowledge directly our commitment to one another. Never to admit the fact that we count on one another *first*. We were never to recognize this in the face of el hombre. But this is what being a Chicana feminist means—making bold and political the love of the women of our race. Possibly the words of one Latina to another will come closer to the cultural/female connection I am trying to describe:

> There is something I feel for you or with you or from you that I experience with no one else, that I need and crave, that I never get enough of, that I do not understand, that I am missing at this very moment... perhaps it's spiritual openness, two souls touching, love that transcends the boundaries of materiality, ordinary reality and living.[23]

No one else can or will speak for us. We must be the ones to define the parameters of what it means to be female and mestiza.

A political commitment to women does not equate with lesbianism. As a Chicana lesbian, I write of the connection my own feminism has had with my sexual desire for women. This is my story. I can tell no other one than the one I understand. I eagerly await the writings by heterosexual Chicana feminists that can speak of their sexual desire for men and the ways in which their feminism informs that desire. What is true, however, is that a political commitment to women must involve, by definition, a political commitment to lesbians as well. To refuse to allow the Chicana lesbian the right to the free expression of her own sexuality, and her politicization of it, is in the deepest sense to deny one's self the right to the same. I guarantee you, there will be no change among heterosexual men, there will be no change in heterosexual relations, as long as the Chicano community keeps us lesbians and gay men political prisoners among our own people. Any movement built on the fear and loathing of anyone is a failed movement. The Chicano movement is no different.

The secret agenda of denial which has so often turned the relationships between mother and daughter, sister and sister, and compañeras into battlegrounds has got to come to an end.

For you, mamá, I have unclothed myself before a woman
have laid wide the space between my thighs
straining open the strings held there
taut and ready to fight.

Stretching my legs and imagination so open
to feel my whole body cradled
by the movement of her mouth, the mouth
of her thighs rising and falling, her arms
her kiss, all the parts of her open
like lips moving, talking me into loving.

I remember this common skin, mamá
oiled by work and worry.
Hers is a used body like yours
one that carries the same scent
of silence   I call it home.

The first women I loved were the women of my race. I
had to go a long ways away de mi pueblo para hallar expresión de
mi amor para la mujer, pero ahora...ahora...

El Regreso a mi pueblo. A la Mujer Mestiza.

EPILOGUE: LA MUJER QUE VIENE DE LA BOCA

There resides in her, as in me, a woman far greater than
our bodies
can inhabit
So I stay
and take what I can
in thick drops
like oil that leaks

from the cave of anger
wrestling between her legs.

Women agitate my consciousness. What I am willing to
work out on paper/in life has always been prompted by women:
la mujer en mi alma, mis sueños—dark, Latina, lover, mother.
Tengo miedo.

In conclusion, quiero decir that these changes scare me.
Returning to la mujer scares me, re-learning Spanish scares me.
I have not spoken much of la lengua here. It is not so much that I
have been avoiding it, only that the conclusion brings me to the
most current point in time: la lengua.

In returning to the love of my race, I must return to the fact
that not only has the mother been taken from me, but her tongue,
her mothertongue. I want the language, feel my tongue rise to
the occasion of feeling at home, in common. I know this language
in my bones...and then it escapes me..."You don't belong.
¡Quítate!"

Journal Entry: 1 de septiembre 1981
*I called up Berlitz today. The Latino who answered refused to
quote me prices over the phone. "Come down and talk to Mr.
Bictner," he says. I want to know how much it's going to cost **before**
I do any train riding into Manhattan. "Send me a brochure," I say,
regretting the call.*

*Paying for culture. When I was born between the legs of the best
teacher I could have had.*

Quiero decir that I know on the surface of things, this is not
to make any sense. I spoke English at home. On the surface of
things I am not supposed to feel that my language has been
stripped from me—I am "born American." College English
educated, but what I must admit is that I have felt in my writing
that the English was not cutting it. ¿Entiendes? That there is
something else, deep and behind my heart and I want to hold it
hot and bold in the hands of my writing and it will not come out
sounding like English. Te prometo. No es inglés. And I have to
wonder, is it so that I have felt "too much," "too emotional," "too
sensitive" because I was trying to translate my feelings into
English cadences?

Mi amiga says to me, she could never go back to not fucking in Spanish. And I think about this. Yo recuerdo a Carmela—su mano trazando los círculos de mis senos around and around bringing her square small hands down, moving my legs apart, opening my lips hovering, holding me there—her light breath on my thighs. No me lame, pero espera, mirandome, diciendo. "¡Qué rica! ¡Ay mujer, qué rica tú eres!"

And I can't quite believe my ears, she is talking about the taste of me *before* su boca lo sabe. She knows *before* hand and mouth make it possible. She tells me my name, my taste, in Spanish. She fucks me in Spanish.

Quiero decirte, re-learning Spanish scares me. I feel like the same and a different woman in Spanish. A different kind of passion. I think, *soy mujer en español*. No macha. Pero Mujer. Soy Chicana—open to all kinds of attack.

In recent months, I have had a recurring dream that my mouth is too big to close; that is, the *outside* of my mouth, my lips, cannot contain the inside—teeth, tongue, gums, throat. I am coming out of my mouth, so to speak. The mouth is red like blood; and the teeth, like bones, white. The skeleton of my feelings clattering for attention.

Returning from the Latin American Women Writer's Conference, I say to my friends as I drive down 91 South, "The Mouth is like a cunt."

La boca spreads its legs open to talk, open to attack. "I am a lesbian. And I am a Chicana," I say to the men and women at the conference. I watch their faces twist up on me. "These are two inseparable facts of my life. I can't talk or write about one without the other."

My mouth cannot be controlled. It will flap in the wind like legs in sex, not driven by the mind. It's as if la boca were centered on el centro del corazón, not in the head at all. The same place where the cunt beats.

And there is a woman coming out of her mouth.

Hay una mujer que viene de la boca.

March 1983

NOTES

1. Norma Alarcón examines this theme in her article, "Chicana's Feminist Literature: A Re-Vision Through Malintzin/or Malintzin: Putting Flesh Back on the Object," in *This Bridge Called My Back: Writings by Radical Women of Color*, eds. Cherríe Moraga and Gloria Anzaldúa (Watertown, MA: Persephone Press, 1981) n.p.

2. Aleida R. Del Castillo, "Malintzin Tenepal: A Preliminary Look into a New Perspective," in *Essays on La Mujer*, eds. Rosaura Sánchez and Rosa Martínez Cruz (University of California at Los Angeles: Chicano Studies Center Publications, 1977) p. 133.

3. *ibid.*, p. 131.

4. *ibid.*, p. 141.

5. Gloria Anzaldúa, unpublished work-in-progress. Write: The Third World Women's Archives, Box 159, Bush Terminal Station, Brooklyn, NY 11232

6. Silvia S. Lizarraga, "From A Woman to A Woman," in *Essays on La Mujer, op. cit.*, p. 91.

7. Alfredo Mirandé and Evangelina Enríquez, *La Chicana: The Mexican-American Woman* (University of Chicago Press, 1979) p. 225.

8. Some future writings by Latina feminists include: Gloria Anzaldúa's *La Serpiente Que Se Come Su Cola: The Autobiography of a Chicana Lesbian* (Write: The Third World Women's Archives, see address above); *Cuentos: Stories by Latinas*, eds. Alma Gómez, Cherríe Moraga, and Mariana Romo-Carmona (Kitchen Table: Women of Color Press, Box 2753 Fockefeller Center Station, New York, NY, 10185, 1983); and, *Compañeras: Antología Lesbiana Latina*, eds. Juanita Ramos and Mirtha Quintanales (Write: The Third World Women's Archives, see address above).

9. The Combahee River Collective, "A Black Feminist Statement," in *But Some of Us Are Brave: Black Women's Studies*, eds. Gloria T. Hull, Patricia Bell Scott, and Barbara Smith (Old Westbury, NY: The Feminist Press, 1982) p. 16.

10. Toni Cade Bambara, *The Salt Eaters* (New York: Random House, 1980) p.3 and p. 10.

11. Bernal Díaz del Castillo, *The Bernal Diaz Chronicles* trans. and ed. Albert Idell (New York: Doubleday, 1956) p. 86-87.

12. Sonia A. López, in *Essays on La Mujer, op. cit.,* p. 26.

13. Norma Alarcón, in *This Bridge Called My Back, op. cit.,* p. 184.

14. Octavio Paz, *The Labyrinth of Solitude: Life and Thought in Mexico* (NY: Grove Press, 1961) p. 77.

15. Cherríe Moraga, "Played Between White Hands," in *Off Our Backs*, July 1982, Washington, D.C. n.p.

16. Mirtha Quintanales with Barbara Kerr, "The Complexity of Desire: Conversations on Sexuality and Difference," in *Conditions: Eight*, Box 56 Van Brunt Station, Brooklyn, NY, p. 60.

17. Bernice Reagon, "Turning the Century Around" in *Home Girls: A Black Feminist Anthology*, ed. Barbara Smith (Brooklyn, NY: Kitchen Table: Women of Color Press, 1983).

18. Barbara Smith, unpublished paper. (Write: Kitchen Table: Women of Color Press, see address above).

19. Combahee River Collective, *op. cit.,* p. 13.

20. *ibid.,* p. 18.

21. Barbara Smith, unpublished paper, *op. cit.*

22. Audre Lorde, *Uses of the Erotic. The Erotic as Power.* (Brooklyn, NY: Out & Out Books, 1978).

23. Mirtha Quintanales, unpublished letter.

En el sueño mi amor me pregunta " Donde está tu río?" And I point to the middle of my chest.

I am a river cracking open. It's as if the parts of me were before just thin tributaries. Lines of water like veins running barely beneath the soil or skimming the bone surface of the earth—sometimes desert creek, sometimes city-wash, sometimes like sweat sliding down a woman's breastbone.

Now I can see the point of juncture. Comunión. And I gather my forces to make the river run.

FEED THE MEXICAN BACK INTO HER

para mi prima

what I meant to say to her as she reached
around the cocktail glass to my hand, squeezing it
    saying, *it makes no difference to me*. what I meant to say
        is that it must make a difference,
        but then I did say that and it made
        no difference, this difference
        between us.

what I meant to say to her is I dreamed we were children. I meant
to tell her how I took her thin brown hand in mine and led her to
the grocery store—the corner one, like in l.a. on adams street,
where I remember her poor and more mexican than ever. we both
were. I meant to remind her of how she looked in her brother's
hand-me-downs—the thin striped tee shirt, the suspenders
holding up the corduroy pants, literally "in suspension" off her
small frame.

I meant to sit her down and describe to her the love, the care with
which I drew the money from my pocket—my plump pink hand,
protective, counting out the change. I bought tortillas, chiles
verdes. I meant to say, "Teresita, mi'jita, when we get home, I'll
make you a meal you'll never forget."

Feed the Mexican back into her.

I meant to tell her how I thought of her as not brown at all, but
black—an english-speaking dark-girl, wanting to spit the white
words out of her—be black angry. I meant to encourage.

Teresita

there is a photograph of us
at seven, you are skinny
at the knees where the brown wrinkles
together black,
my hand like a bright ring around yours

we are smiling.

In the negative, I am dark
and profane/you light & bleached-boned
my guts are grey & black coals glowing.

I meant to say, *it is* this *fire you see*
coming out from inside me.

Call it the darkness you still wear
on the edge of your skin
the light you reach for
across the table
and into my heart.

AND THEN THERE'S US

for LaRue and Elvira

Nobody would believe it
to look at us

how our families'
histories
converge.

> Two women on opposite south
> ends of the continent
> working cotton
> for some man.

> Nobody would believe it.

> Their backs
> and this country
> collapsing

> to make room for us together.

QUERIDA COMPAÑERA

"...fue como rencontrar una parte de mi misma que estaba
perdida, fue el reafirmar mi amor por las mujeres, por la mujer,
por mi raza, mi lengua, el amor que me debo a mi misma..."
                              —una carta de mi compañera, mayo 1982

¿qué puedo decirte in return
stripped of the tongue
that could claim lives
de otras perdidas?

la lengua que necesito
para hablar
es la misma que uso
para acariciar

tú sabes.
you know the feel of woman
lost en su boca
        amordazada

it has always been like this.

profundo y sencillo
lo que nunca
pasó
por sus labios

but was
        utterly
        utterly
        heard.

GLOSSARY

p. ii, line 15
our suffering in the world
line 27
kisses to the portrait

p. iii, lines 4-5
my aunts in procession arriving at my grandmother's door each
day
line 8
they are fighting
line 10
the lies
line 16
She'll be crying. Again.
lines 19-21
My grandmother is dying very slowly. She closes her eyes. She
closes her mouth. The hospital gives her food through the veins.
She doesn't speak. She doesn't sing like she used to.
line 22
the shadow of her own death
lines 23-24
She is sleeping, waiting for death.

p. iv. lines 4-5
In the dream, I was trying to take a picture of my grandmother
and mother. Meanwhile a woman was waiting for me in the bed.
line 10
Later I dreamed about my brother. He has returned to the family.

p. v. line 20
the risk always lives

p. vi. lines 10-11
"You need to travel to see what community really is."

p. vii, lines 19-20
"Grandma? Do you recognize me? I just got in from New York?
lines 23-24
"I'm hungry! I want chorizo! I'm so hungry!"

line 26
"Where's your mother?"
line 27
"Here I am, mother."
line 28
"And JoAnn, is she here too?"
line 29
"Yes grandma. I'm here and Erin."

p. viii. lines 2-3
The line of women, the family root. My mother is so proud at this moment.
lines 7-8
The death of my grandmother. And I never spoke to her in the language she could understand.

p. 11, lines 4-5
"Do you understand? But don't tell your sister anything."
line 32
"He's ashamed."

p. 37, lines 16-17
Who knows the pain this woman has endured?
lines 22-23
"The shit of the world that eats shit!"

p. 45, line 1
But that's a dream.

p. 140, lines 24-25
from my people in order to find expression of my love for women, but now...now...
line 26
The return to my people. To the Mestiza Woman.

p. 141, line 5
the woman in my soul, my dreams
line 6
I'm afraid.
line 17
"Get out of here!"

p. 142, lines 2-3
I remember Carmela, her hand tracing the circles of my breasts.
    line 6
She doesn't lick me, but waits, looking at me, saying,
    line 32
the center of the heart

p. 149, line 5
what can I tell you
    line 8
of others lost
    lines 9-12
the tongue/need/to speak/is the same/use/to touch
    lines 15-16
in her muzzled/mouth
    lines 18-21
simple and profound/what never/passed/through her lips

Cherríe Moraga is a Chicana poet and "politica," born in Los Angeles, California in 1952. She is presently living in New York where she helped found, and is an active member of, Kitchen Table: Women of Color Press.